PREPARING PREACHERS TO PREACH

Preparing Preachers To Preach

By

R. AMES MONTGOMERY

President of Lane Seminary
Professor of Homiletics in the Presbyterian
Theological Seminary, Chicago

ZONDERVAN PUBLISHING HOUSE
GRAND RAPIDS   MICHIGAN

EIGHT-FIFTEEN FRANKLIN STREET
GRAND RAPIDS, MICHIGAN

To

JOHN MARTIN AND FRANCES CAROLINE WRIGHT MONTGOMERY
WHO FOR FORTY-FIVE YEARS SERVED HOME MISSION
CHURCHES IN INDIANA AND OHIO

ACKNOWLEDGMENT

The author desires to acknowledge his indebtedness to the authors and publishers whose works are cited in the "Notes" of this volume. (Pages 245-249)

FOREWORD

"THE highest qualification of a preacher is to have a message from God for the weary, longing heart of man. His effective ministry waits for the declaiming of this good news, and this vindication of God in the energy and ongoing resources and disposition of the world. The church calls today for men with a message. She waits for men with a superior life to live and a burning faith to declare—for men with a life that will so exceed the common life that it will put to shame all that is of mere prudence and calculation, and give hope for despair. She knows what she wants, and is ready to honor the herald."[1]

"Many preachers demur against the uniform require-ment of all these parts as necessary members of a sermon. They would claim a discretion to omit all of them except the argument, and perhaps the conclusion. They say our requirement is mischievously formal, and dictates a tiresome sameness. They deprecate such ser-mons as 'casts all run in the same mold.' Let me then, in advance explain. Their sarcasm suggests an unjust analogy. Sermons are not dead casts run into any mold, changeable or fixed. Give a new mold for each attempt, to be demolished when once used; I still reject and resent the illustration. Sermons should be living growths, like plants or trees; none of them indeed mon-sters, none maimed, but each one modified within the bounds of the rudimental laws of its nature, by its own circumstances of growth; so that they together present an endless and charming variety. Every natural tree must needs have certain constituent parts—its roots, its stem, its branches, its foliage, its fruit. But how endlessly diversified is the development of these members! They cannot any of them be wholly absent, but the individuality of each tree determines their relative size; so that we have very graceful differences of form and stature, from the humble shrub to the tapering and lofty pine. This is the model toward which every sermon, even the most informal, must tend."[2]

TABLE OF CONTENTS

CHAPTER I

THE ECLIPSE AND RELUMINATION OF PREACHING

FOR MANY years preaching has been passing through an eclipse. Thirty-five years ago, a great religious and social weekly published a series of articles on "Why I Left the Ministry." One of the articles declared a "preacher's opinions were of no more value than the opinions of a pretty woman," by which the writer of it meant they had reached the zero point. Years ago the impatience of the campus resounded with "Don't preach to me"—a contemptible procedure in the mind of the student.

Dr. William Chalmers Covert, in 1934, in his book, *Facing Our Day*,[1] observes "doubt and discouragement in the ministry. Men here and there have lost from their calling the certification of their own self-assurance. Sometimes the cynical spirit creeps into the heart as they face the cant, the hypocrisy, and moral cowardice about them."

Within a short time we have had the nonplussed suggestion of Dr. Fleming that "we declare a moratorium for two years."

Year by year the numbers of churches abandoning

11

the evening worship-hours increase. The problem of
"holding the young people" grows more acute, while
the preacher is held more and more responsible for
their loss. Preachers themselves lack clarity and
unanimity of conviction as to what is their function
in this complex, sophisticated, and muddled generation. Public concern for what the preacher says seems
to fade.

Such facts indicate the situation in which the eclipse
of preaching is presented to us. Two factors are involved: the message and the man. In suggesting a
way of escape and a relumination of preaching, two
questions arise:

1. What brought this about?
2. What can be done to reluminate preaching?

It is with these two factors and the attempt to answer
these two questions we are concerned.

Let us begin with a recognition of this fact. *Preaching has been thrown into this eclipse by the prodigious
influence of what we call the "new science."* Enough
for us now to recognize this fact and just to ask how
it came to affect preaching. In answer we say, the new
science produced an atmosphere unfriendly to preaching. Because of what science has done to increase the
wealth and comfort, the health and amusement of the
people, it commands their attention. It has satisfied
them with the world in which they live. Science has
enabled the people to get rich quickly and with less
effort. If they have more than they can store, it tells
them to tear down their barns and build greater. It
adds no warning of the dangers that beset them while
doing this.

Science has taught the people to believe that by study

and understanding of the laws of the natural world they can make gadgets, which by the turn of a dial or the push of a button, will shed light on every dark situation with which they can possibly be perplexed. It has banished many mysteries. Many people believe there are no mysteries science will not ultimately pierce in the present or the hereafter. Science has made the rich richer and more comfortable. It has provided bread and circus for the poor; and the people are satisfied.

While scientists are beginning to discover the limitations and the prostitutions to which science is subject, these facts are not publicized so widely as were their successes. It will probably be a long time before the public knows of or is impressed by these limitations— if it ever knows. Limitations are not news. As for the prostitutions of science—they pay huge dividends.

In the second place, the scientific method and procedure were applied to religion. When thus applied to the sources of the Christian faith, they shook it to its foundations. Students of religious data too often seemed to have a greater deference toward science than they had toward religion. Some of us can remember with what laughter and applause a certain popular pulpit presentation of critical conclusions about the Book of Jonah was greeted and so reported in the Metropolitan press, forty years ago. It helped to develop the atmosphere in which frivolity and cynicism flourished and in which preaching was discredited. When the attention was turned to the Gospels, to use a phrase of a great weekly journal, "The battle raged about the standard," and scattered and confused the multitude. Religion was badly dealt with in the minds of preachers and people. The unfriendly atmosphere scientific agencies created was heightened by this attack on religious sources.

In this conflict and unfriendly atmosphere, preachers lost their vitality and zeal of conviction. They lost confidence in the trustworthiness of the sources of their faith. The materials of their message were depreciated. The warrant for their vocation was questioned. There was a time around the close of the last century when many felt the foundations were being destroyed, and if the foundations be destroyed, what shall the righteous do? We are now well out of that portion of the eclipse, but we must not forget many are still in the shadow. Spectres of that night still haunt large sections of the people—many of them in our educational institutions. The air is not warm and friendly there, but cold and chilling. The pity of it is that, with many preachers, there lingers a timidity and fear that modifies their ardor of conviction. They have to pick and choose their Scripture portions. They fear the Christian tradition is impaired. No less so, doubts and questionings remain with the people. If they are questioned as to which they deem the most competent *leaders* for the people, scientists or clergy, they would vote for scientists. Preaching does not flourish in such environment.

We do not forget the considerations for encouragement. Splendid personalities in science still believe the gospel and hug its blessed consolations to their bosom. They bravely witness their loyalty to the Christian message. But the weight of their testimony for religion is largely canceled by an open confession that from the standpoint of science, some vital elements in religion *cannot be proved*. So like the faint praise that damns, their testimony lends no power in our efforts to meet the opposition. But how eagerly do we preachers listen to the scientists, and how confidently do we recount their words intended to encourage us! We ought to do this. It may help to create a new atmosphere. It will *not lead* to a renaissance of Christian faith. We must remember our cause does not depend upon scientific approval.

Again, in the gift of bread and the circus to the multitudes, in the increase of wealth and comforts to the rich, that science brought, the ministry was too much beguiled into thinking bread and the circus, riches and comforts were necessities of existence. We shared in prosperity and lost our vision. Large numbers of preachers sat at tables where science brought the viands and the rich spread the table. Some fared sumptuously every day. They forgot, "man shall not live by bread alone." Many will deny this and declare they did not forget. But they put their faith in such stocks on the market as belie their statement. Preachers were dazed, if not blinded to the truth, that "the things that are seen are temporal, but that which is not seen is eternal." It took a world cataclysm of stocks and bonds to awaken many preachers to the fact, and to recall them to the words of Jesus—"Where a man's treasure is, there will his heart be also."

Two incidents are recalled of nearly twenty years ago. One is a conversation with a Baptist preacher whose salary was not increased when his people were growing rich. Said he, "Montgomery, the prophet is usually a hungry man." The other—the words of an old missionary mother who never had more than seven hundred and fifty dollars a year on which to raise her family. Her eldest son had been called to a pastorate paying the enormous salary of twenty-four hundred dollars a year and she lovingly warned him not to be drawn away by the love of the world and the lust thereof.

But how easily this thing happens! How easy for ministers getting the prosperity the world brings to use judgment-values it begets. How naturally they begin to look on the brethren whose income is small as getting all they are worth. Nothing blurs the prophet's vision and warps his judgment like hobnobbing with prosperity. Fear of the intellectuals and the prosperous, fear of poverty for themselves, present spectres that kill courage and valiancy in prophets. Many preachers were put in eclipse between 1918 and 1929 by these things.

But, to return to the atmosphere to which we have previously referred. In this atmosphere that science made for the world and for religion, not only the preachers lost an estimate of spiritual values, but their people did also and especially as assets for preaching. No man can escape this who has been frequently consulted by church committees seeking ministers for their vacant pulpits. What congregations seem to want in their preachers is the energy of the flesh, which is the possession of youth; sociability, which is the possession of those eager to get on; organizing skill, the talent for those who are of the machine age; men of easy address, which is not always the possession of the thoughtful. In reviewing an experience comprehensive in time and places it is interesting to note how infrequently committees showed any anxiety to find a man who knew his Bible and Jesus Christ as Savior and Lord. What they wanted was a "go-getter type" of man who is the idol of a commercial age. But there were few inquiries showing concern for great preaching—character-developing preaching, soul-saving preaching; to use Faber's words, preaching "touchy for the interests of Jesus." Not more than once or twice in years was such preaching sought.

Of course, preaching cannot be developed in an age that has lowered its standards so much. It cannot expect development to normal, let alone distinguished proportions, in such an eclipse of faith and life.

The second great factor that has affected preaching is mechanistic psychology. I refer to the teaching of such men as James H. Leuba (b. 1868), J. B. Watson (b. 1878), Robert Chenault Givler (b. 1884), and Joseph Wood Krutch (b. 1893), all instructors in well known and highly accredited colleges located in various sections of the country from the Atlantic to the Pacific during their teaching career. There are others, but these represent the psychology referred to. The teaching of these respective individuals is wholly at variance with the Christian concept of the nature of man, of human personality and its ethical demands. Being popular propagandists, by voice and pen, their influence has gone far beyond the locus of their personal and professional contacts. So effective have they been, wherever men of Christian conviction have expressed themselves on the subject of Christian education for our youth, they have been in disagreement with the teachings of those men and warned their students and readers against their mechanistic teaching. However, their influence has gone abroad. The implication of their mechanistic theories is wholly adverse to Christian preaching and the Christian concept of life. To adapt the language of Krutch relative to "Humanism" and "Nature," we may say, their concepts "have been frequently employed rather because of certain affective connotations than because of any exact meaning."[2] Because of their reputation as scientists, or philosophers, and their bold assault upon the traditional order, these men have been far more effective upon the public mind than most preachers are aware. The minds and hearts of Christian multitudes have been chilled by them, and Christian teachings have been deflected from many others who have never heard a word from their lips nor read a page from their books. They created an atmosphere. Their influence on concepts of Christian personality has been devastating. From a generation living in such an atmosphere, we get little response to a teaching that "God created man in His own image, in the image of God created He him." Such a generation lives blithely and cynically on a plane far below that on which the messenger of God stands and appeals.

One effect of this mechanistic psychology and its philosophy can be traced in a weakened emphasis on personality values as a primary asset desirable in messengers of the gospel. Observation of selective processes leads to the conviction that the inquiries into personality qualifications of ministerial candidates is one of the least considered. The result is, too many have been admitted whose personality gave no promise of capacity for leadership. Too many men have been admitted who gave no promise of being what Dr. Chalmers called "Men of Weight." Those who have read John Oman's *Concerning the Ministry*, will appreciate how important a consideration has been omitted in this neglected emphasis.

A preacher, who at a later period in life became a peripatetic listener, particularly interested in discovering homiletic and personal values, listening to different men in widely separated places, from Podunk to Metropolitan town, is impressed with the deficit in personality that marks the ministry. He gets the conviction that next to not knowing how to preach, many men cannot meet personality values for which the occasion calls.

Some years ago a friend visited me over the week-end. He was a friend of preachers and a loyal churchman, and withal, one of the most successful and influential business men in the great Northwest. We attended one of the largest and best equipped churches in the city. The order of service was acceptable in every part except the preacher's own part. He read the Scriptures without any note of distinction in spirit or interpretation. His prayers gave no evidence of meditation or preparation. He dwelt at length on the announcements, which were commmonplace. When he preached, there was not a single indication of previous preparation. For forty minutes he rambled on o'er barren fields and burnt-over landscapes. At last he came to an end.

When we left the church and walked to the street, my friend turned and looked at the great pile of stone and then said, "Did Dr. Blank build that?" "It was built during his pastorate," I replied. "Is he considered a man of parts?" "Some. Were you disappointed tonight?" "It was very disappointing." Then with an earnest shake of his head, "There is not enough man there."

The difficulty of that situation was not primarily the want of academic or professional curriculum, but a deficit in personality. The preacher was not a man of weight.

I am reminded of another experience. Visiting in a large city on the Sabbath, I had attended the church alone. One of the parishioners invited me to ride home with him. En route the sermon was referred to and soundly criticized. I asked, "Why did you join this church?" "Because," said his wife, "we have tried three others and the preaching is no better there. This church is fairly convenient and Rev. ———— is a like-able person to meet. But," she continued, "if Protestantism doesn't develop more *preachers* it is doomed," to which her husband nodded approval.

As we confront this situation in which preaching has fallen into an eclipse, clear suggestions appear for its relumination. The chapters that follow will indicate the author's belief that the preacher's acquaintance with the principles and techniques of sermon building are of first importance. If this is to be gained, definite, intelligent, and adequate instruction must be given in the schools for the training of preachers. It is also highly desirable, when a man's school days are over, that he have, in usable form, such instruction in a volume readily at hand to which he can turn and revive previous instruction and test his own progress and output occasionally. More important than this, perhaps, is the preparation of the *man himself*. Books that record the experience of those who have gone the way he now travels, that tell something of what the author has learned in the school of hard knocks, ought to be both informing and inspiring.

Beyond the preacher, there are responsibilities that rest upon the whole church and particularly upon those who meet candidates at the point of life where they start on the road of "whole-time Christian service" in the ministry.

It, therefore, seems desirable to indicate the emphasis persons acting as the representatives of the whole church should make in selecting young men for the work of preaching. Bishops, conferences, associations, and presbyterial committees are too often disposed to take the testimony of interested pastors or people, proud of their candidate for the gospel ministry, without discharging their duty in an adequate examination of the candidate himself and in an observation of the personality values he may or may not possess. *Personality values ought to be given primary consideration* when young men *are enrolled as candidates for the gospel ministry.* In this, the most complex, confused, irreverently critical and still grossly ignorant age, so far as problems of spiritual leadership are concerned, all are agreed, no factor bulks so big as that we describe as personality. We agree with John Oman, "When God gives some prophets, it means that He sends them with natural endowments of insight and courage and forceful character, telling speech and intrepid action, as well as faith and peace and love, and the weight of the message depends largely on the weight of the ambassador. No doubt this included ability, but it mainly concerned depth and force of character. Without it can anyone be truly a prophet? For any ministry among the gifts which are a call to it, this one of personal weight ought to be in the forefront. Nothing counts so much in preaching, at least for enduring impression, nor, for that matter, in any part of a man's ministry."[3]

Therefore, some principles must be discovered and used for the estimate of personality values in candidates for the ministry. These should be applied when the candidates are initially considered. We are greatly encouraged in the steps already taken by the theological leaders and the denominational boards of education. The selection of such principles, and the method of procedure in using them, will require wisdom and judgment in human and religious values not many academic personages possess. When once these principles and methods of procedure are adopted, it will take time to get them accepted by the ministers and congregation presenting the candidate. But we may begin, perhaps, by asking whether this man gives promise of developing that weight which the impact of effective preaching requires, instead of dwelling entirely on the fact that he attends Christian Endeavor regularly.

Secondly, we must recover our emphasis on *personal experience of a vital relation to Christ*. Thomas Carlyle said, "Soul is kindled only by soul, and to teach religion the one thing needful is to find a man who has religion."[4] Effective preaching depends upon the preacher's knowledge and experience of the gospel. He may be able to quote long passages from memory, or locate proof-texts supporting creeds, or even lecture extensively on the contents of the Bible before intellectual or moral savants; he may be able to talk well about the life and ministry of the Carpenter of Nazareth and yet never utter a phrase so that his utterance indicates he knows Him. There is a difference in the language of the man who has worked out his problems in the laboratory and the man whose talk is only out of what he has read about it. There is authority in the word, "We know we have passed from death unto life, because we love the brethren," as they fall from the lips of a man who *loves* the brethren. Such a man demonstrates it in a sacrificial attitude, spirit, and action in human contacts. He surrenders opportunities for them. He seeks to promote their interests. His opposite does not love men, however much talk and activities in benevolent language and enterprise may be indulged. This experience of the gospel truth is fundamental to real preaching. It is what John Henry Jowett called a "passion for souls." The sexton of one of the churches Jowett served knew Jowett for just that. He loved his fellow-men. On two occasions, we went to hear him and could not get in. Placards announced all seats and standing-room taken. Then the sexton's story about Jowett's love for men enabled us to understand it. He had experimental knowledge of Christ's love for men. People want to hear such a man.

That "certificate of self-assurance" Dr. Covert and many others bemoan as lost in the ministry, may be recovered just in proportions as ministers advance in this experience of the truth in Christ. This brings to an audience the conviction that such a man is not talking to promote church attendance or his own popularity. They soon learn such a man wants to save their souls. Such a preacher seldom reminds people, "Thus saith the Lord." He does not need to. They know it, because they have heard him say it whose utterance and life demonstrate it.

In the third place, let me suggest *the Bible must be restored to a place of authority in preaching from*

which it fell when we got rid of an inspired Book.
Men who rejoiced in getting rid of an inspired Book
as well as an inspired church, did not do much to get
preaching out of its eclipse. They only brought to the
generations first to receive their conclusions an impairment of the sources on which preaching most depended
for a preaching message. As it got abroad that the
Bible was not "inspired," it naturally followed that texts
began to be ignored. Many ceased to use them. The
more daring and capable men thought well upon the
problems of life and offered their opinions on these
problems in acceptable language and challenging
concepts of thought. But their followers in too many
instances could not do that. Neglecting the great compendium of human history in moral and religious
conflicts, they could not see these values in current life;
consequently, their opinions were not worth much. They
brought to their pulpit only dead coals. Fire could
not be kindled with these, it mattered not how hard
they blew upon them. Thoughtful men began to discover the pulpit fire was out and however much they
needed its warmth and comfort it was not worth while
to look to the pulpit to be warmed.

Preachers tried to make up for this by increased
presentation of social theories, economic utterances, and
moral platitudes. This only brought contempt from men
who needed guidance. Then preachers became hys-
terical in mixing with the people they had lost. They
became Rotarians, Lions, Optimists, Kiwanians, club
men of every description — anything to demonstrate
they were good fellows. They ran from one meeting
to another in social and civic enterprises. They had
no time for study, prayer, or meditations. They be-

came "good mixers." When the end of the week came they sat down to write their sermons for Sunday mornings; but when they brought their engagements of the week to the pulpit, they brought strange fire. They were not dealing religiously with the bosom and business of men. When they talked on social situations, economic conditions, and political corruptions, they were outdone by men whose business it was to deal with such things and who knew what they were talking about. When they quoted authorities in sociology, economics, politics, and business, the thoughtful preacher's audience had already read what he had said.

What the people wanted from their preacher was something they called a "religious message." Too often they did not get it. Why should they go to hear secondhand stuff from a preacher? Whatever the preacher might say about God and His relation to them found them. Forgiveness, prayer, redemption from sin, hope of life to come, searched the nooks and crannies of the soul. It threw a flood of light on dark places. It inspired them to hope. It girded them for life's battles. These Bible subjects are the subjects they want to hear their preacher talk about. Multitudes have wondered why their preacher does not bring messages on these great matters.

If we are to come out of this eclipse and relumine preaching, preachers must return to a definite, specific conviction that there are in the Bible values that the human mind and heart need, and without the meeting of this need, the will can never be implemented in great Christian living. The preacher must deal with these Scriptures earnestly and practically. The chief exponent of preaching without a text, Dr. Harry Emerson Fosdick, preacher for the Sunday Evening Club, Chicago, April 4, 1937, never did a better piece of work than he did on that occasion. But he had a text, and he unfolded its deep meanings to the great audience that heard him. Preachers must treat their Scripture with more respect than as a peg to hang their personal opinions on. They must unfold the great teachings of these Scriptures. They must do it confidently, sincerely, passionately, as men who have tried and proved their worth in a life they have shared with their congregations. They must throw the Bible's light on life's dark places.

Finally, *preaching must recover the power of appeal.* What is preaching and what is the preacher trying to do? Preaching is primarily the utterance of a testimony and conviction. This utterance is intended to lead men and women to become Christ-like in personality and conduct. No generation has been nor can be saved by literary essays and interesting statements of historical values. A preacher who knows his business seeks a verdict in his preaching. He wants a decision that leads to definite action or course of life. This he cannot get unless he clearly defines to himself what he wants and so addresses himself to the personality of his hearers. The result he seeks must be based upon an intelligent understanding, accompanying emotions, and a movement of the wills of the persons addressed.

Preachers have been intimidated respecting their address to the emotions. It is said, "This is taking unfair advantage when you appeal to the emotions. Intelligent people resent such appeals." "It is not dignified, when preaching to intelligent hearers, either to exhort or plead." "Whatever you do, do not let the preacher get

excited about religion or anybody getting it." Too
many preachers are like the Episcopal clergyman who
told the happy hallelujah Negro woman, "The church
is no place to get religion" (of the emotional type).
Those intimidated shun any appeal to the emotions.
They take the calm attitude of the proverbial lecturer
or instructor to a class in mathematics or physics. "Ap-
pealing to the intellect is the way to win people." Such
preachers should read and remember the statement of
the Hon. Oliver Wendell Holmes to Dr. John C. Wu,
"I hate to discourage the belief of the young in reason.
I believe in it with all my heart, but I think that its
control over the actions of men when it comes against
what they want is not very great." Just so. Such an
address does not move the will.

The Presbyterian Church lost so much by essay and
lecture-types of preaching that its leadership became
alarmed back in the nineties. J. Wilbur Chapman was
appointed executive secretary on evangelism to awaken
the church and recover the loss of appeal in preaching.
The situation, far broader than the Presbyterian Church,
was not much improved by it. Some of us who ought
to have been shot several years ago after the advice of
a great medical joker about it, but were not, have now
to brouse around in many pastures. Is it strange if we,
listening now, make some discoveries? Among these
is the discovery that many preachers make no address
to the emotions and no appeal to become Christ-like.
Too many seem to feel that their sermon is something
to be "delivered," but for what purpose, "deponent saith
not." People may take it or leave it—the preacher will
lose no sleep.

My brothers, this ought not to be. Men must plead

the cause of Christ. Plead for action, for decision, for loyalty, and service upon a definite instruction to the conscience. We have to take the citadel of man's soul. It can be done only by a disciplined utterance of the truth, and a wooing, pleading appeal to those who hear.

The new day for preaching will come when men become as zealous for Christ as they are desirous for place and power, which desire, Dick Shepherd said, is in the blood of all the churches. It is the writer's personal conviction, when this power of appeal returns, the eclipse of preaching will pass and the relumination of preaching will begin.

CHAPTER II

THE TEXT

IN THE PREPARATION of men to preach they should be thoroughly trained in the technique of the art. The sermon is a very human thing. It ought to represent a man at his best. When we begin to take it apart to see how it is made, we are often disappointed, because in the analysis we are not able to discover the secret of its beauty or power in the sermon as seen and felt when listening to the preaching of it. Life seems to have gone out of it in the process of analysis. It is like working with a scalpel on a living thing. When you put the knife in, life departs.

Nevertheless, to learn how to preach, one has to learn how to build the message. To be a doctor, a man has to know anatomy. So with him who would be a preacher. He has to know the parts of a sermon and what function they serve. Every sermon has its constituent parts. There are laws, architechtonic in character, which every sermon builder ought to know. The different parts have rules and principles governing them.

In examining the constituent parts of a sermon, we begin with the text:

The Text is that portion of the Scripture on which the preacher's message is founded. "But," you may say, "does a man need to take a text to build a sermon,

to preach?" Some of the most popular preachers seldom, or never, use a text. Some of the greatest teachers
say it is not necessary to take a text.

That great French homilete, Alexander Vinet, says,
"I do not consider the employment of a text essential
to the discourse from the pulpit. And in reality it
is not. What makes a sermon Christian is not the employment of a text but the spirit of the preacher. A
sermon may be Christian, edifying, instructive, without confining itself within the limits of a passage of
Holy Scripture. It may also be quite Scriptural without
having a text, just as with a text it may be by no means
Scriptural. A passage of Scripture has a thousand times
served for a passport to ideas, which were Scriptural;
and we have seen preachers make for themselves, as
it were, a kind of sport, by putting as the head of their
composition a very strong Biblical text, in order to give
themselves the pleasure of enervating them."[1]

This statement for the non-textual sermon is as
strongly put as anyone has made it. Yet, as stated,
there are several things to be said in rebuttal. We
agree that a preacher's utterance may be "Christian,
instructive, and edifying without a text," but it may,
also, not be a sermon. It may be a "talk," or a lecture,
or an oration. We may agree that the spirit of the
preacher must be Christian; but that does not mean
that everything a Christian preacher proclaims is a
sermon. We do not deny that a Christian preacher
speaks to the public many things in the spirit of Christ
that are not sermons; things that are "edifying," and
"instructive." To speak of a text as limiting and to
make it an argument against the use of it, is not valid.
We acknowledge a text does limit; but failure to ob-

serve those limits invalidates the utterance of many
preachers. The *value* of a text is that it does limit.
An efficient preacher gains in efficiency by the observance of those limits. The old Scotch woman's complaint against her minister was that he took his text
and then "went into all the world and preached the
gospel." Her objection was a valid one. That texts
have been dishonored, as Vinet says they have, is true;
but that is not an argument against the use of them
and their being essential to efficient preaching.

Dr. Fosdick is most frequently cited as America's
non-textual preacher. In a contribution to the subject
of preaching published in Harper's Magazine of July,
1928, Dr. Fosdick contrasts the textual preacher (who
is more interested in what became of the Jebusites than
folk), with the topical preacher (who does not start
with a text, but is more interested in his own ideas than
people), both of whom he correctly observes, miss the
mark. He recognizes the dangers that beset both types
of textual and non-textual preachers. His objection to
the use of the text is that it is a formality that often destroys spontaneity and directness of approach. He follows his method because he thinks it to be historically in
conformity with the early practice among Christian
believers and preachers. These early Christians often
began their sermon by seizing upon some immediate
incident or occasion, timely circumstance, or deeply
spiritual truth and preached Christ. He goes back to the
original meaning and use of the word. *Sermon* meant
"familiar talk," "conversation," or "discussion."

This is a strong position, we readily grant. However,
it is a position that fails to recognize our present situation adequately. *We face audiences in these days*

meagerly acquainted with the Scripture. Many men
and women are members of the organized church who
are not Christian personages. We face a generation that
is so ignorant of the Scriptures it may be said to know
nothing of their content. *Listening to preaching without a text, they are not turned to the source upon which
the message finds its true foundations. They do not
know where to find the truth upon which the Christian
character is built and by which it is directed and
governed. Such persons do not develop into "adventurous" or valiant Christian characters.* They have no data
upon which the law of association for Christian ideas
and thought can operate. They may be deeply stirred
for the hour; but when it is past, there is no word,
or phrase, or sentence from the Book that sticks; that
is like a sword-thrust in the flesh, to awaken and stir
the depths of the soul; that may serve as a guide to
bring them back to God. One of the great tasks confronting preachers demands not only that they convince
men of the Christian truth, but also that they equip
them with a knowledge of it. To do this requires a
definite acquaintance with truth at its primary source,
a citation that will enable them to find it, to become
familiar with it, to get its environment and to breathe
the atmosphere that surrounds it.

We do not deny there are dangers besetting the *announcement* of a text. The habit *is* liable to become
formal and stilted, the expression or words used repe-
titious. The one thing to be said about this is, *do not
allow it to become so.* A wide-awake preacher takes
account of the way other ministers do this. Listening
to the best, he makes a careful note of *what* they say
and *how* they say it. Let him check on the sources

dealt with in his reading and hearing of such men. He will often find that even Dr. Fosdick, very soon after he begins preaching, makes a reference to and quotes a particular utterance of Jesus, or some saying of Paul, or some portion of the Old Testament, which, if he had told his listeners where they would find the reference, they would have a source to turn to that is authoritative, that witnesses to Christ, and which the Spirit of God uses to the saving of men. In the use of such a word the thing all preachers must endeavor to avoid is becoming hackneyed. That is indeed the "besetting sin" in the announcement or introduction of the text.

An objection that is often raised to the announcement of the text is its futility. "In this day people do not believe in or acknowledge the authority of the Bible." Its right to speak to men is questioned in this generation.

This statement of the case may have probably been an exaggeration. However correct or incorrect the statement may be as a statement of fact, the answer is that whether those to whom you preach do or do not believe, is not of first importance. *The question is, do you, the preacher, believe the Bible?* Unless a man does believe and honor it, then it is most likely he can't preach at all, though he may think he can. The man who preaches must have a subject or theme. A theme, we shall discover, is the statement of the essential thought, truth, or message to be presented, which came from somewhere, and which for the Christian preacher came from the Bible or was easily identified with some portion of the Bible. When it is so identified with the Biblical record it will usually be found to have far broader implications than its immediate connections indicate.

Voltaire was among those reputed to condemn texts for preaching and is quoted by Dr. Broadus: "It were to be wished Bourdaloue in banishing from the pulpit the bad taste which disgraced it, had also banished the custom of preaching on a text. Indeed to speak long on a quotation of a line or two, to exhaust oneself in subjecting a whole discourse to the controls of this line, seems a trifling labor, little worthy of the dignity of the ministry. The text becomes a sort of motto, or rather enigma, which the discourse develops."[2]

This "sneer," Dr. Broadus points out is accounted for in the "torturing interpretations so often witnessed" and the critic's lack of reverence for the Bible and ignorance of the preacher's true relation to the Bible. When we consider this objection against the use of Biblical texts in preaching as made in our day, we find it has force only with persons tainted with doubt as to the historical integrity of the Bible or people who have read it but little, whose minds are preoccupied with their current problems to the neglect of their Bibles. These are the people who neglect or deplore textual preaching. Preachers who have neglected their Bibles become timid and cowardly in spirit and are too ready to accept the world's aspersions cast on the Bible. It could be easily proved that the multitudes, learned and unlearned, rich and poor, the high and low, eagerly await the message of the gospel from men who believe their Bibles to be the Word of God; who select their themes most frequently from the Bible, and who found their preaching on the Bible content. The Bible offers the grandest themes; the most challenging themes; the

most authoritative themes. The man who believes and
studies his Bible for its preachable message will find
it incomparable as a source.

While some people present a front of patronizing
superiority toward Bible-textual preaching, on the other
hand, there are multitudes who long for it. There are
still many who hold—"the heavenliness of the matter,
the efficacy of the doctrine, the majesty of the style,
the consent of all the parts, the scope of the whole
(which is to give all glory to God), the full discovery
it makes of the only way of man's salvation, the many
other incomparable excellencies, and the entire perfection thereof, are arguments whereby it doth abundantly evidence itself to be the Word of God."[3] If
so, the messenger of God ought to hearken to it and
proclaim it.

Again, it is said, "If the preacher is confined to
the uniform use of texts he may be cramped or crippled."[4] "There are subjects on which the modern
preacher is bound to speak which are not contained,
except by inference, in the Bible; for example—many
aspects of modern industrial life, democracy, prohibition, and ethical problems that arise in the complex
civilization of today."[5]

It is with some hesitancy one takes issue with as
competent a scholar or as gifted a teacher of homiletics
as Ozora Davis. But after forty years in the ministry,
preaching in churches, shops, schools, at luncheon
clubs, on the street and in city parks upon many aspects
of modern industrial life—democracy, prohibition, and
ethical problems that arise in the complex civilization
of our day—the uniform use of texts has not "left us
cramped or crippled." The Bible has never failed

us with a text for the occasion. We have spoken
without a text; but, on such an occasion we did not
preach or think of our utterance as a sermon. A text
was not demanded and one was not used as a pre-
text or a motto. If a man has any ground for inference, that ground ought to be stated, unless he fears
its evil effect. When a preacher brings his utterance
to the public on controversial subjects he will find
utterance gains force and authority by such a statement of his grounds if they be in the Word of God.

We now consider some *arguments for* the use of the
text in addition to what we said in considering arguments against its use.

First, *the use of a text indicates, at once, the importance of the Scripture to the preacher*. His audience
is informed of its importance. His preaching or his
utterance is indicated as a sermon, not a talk, an essay, lecture, address, or oration. It is a sermon. It
demands his best as a preacher. The continued use
of a text will, sooner or later, convince the most in-
attentive and thoughtless that you base your message
on what you believe is the authority of the Word of
God. Such a man, by diligent and efficient preaching,
gains both a hearing and a respect for himself and the
Word he preaches.

Second, *it is the way for him to become a Scriptural
preacher*. Such a man must be a constant reader and
student of his Bible. As in all teaching, he will discover that this is the most practical and effective way
for him to "know his Bible." He not only becomes
acquainted with the environment of his text but also
with its great doctrines, its lofty visions, its pity, its
tragedy and romance, its prophetic prospects, its en-

listing biographies, its great principles, applicable to
the situation this complex civilization presents.

Third, *he will discover by constant study and use
of definite portions of the Bible, its power and finality,*
in turning men from darkness to light, from sin unto
righteousness, and from the power of Satan unto God.
There is no utterance that has ever fallen from the
lips of men that has equaled the Scriptures for that.
Why? Because in the Book we learn of the things
of Christ which it is the function of the Holy Spirit
to make effective for the saving of men. In His hands
it becomes the agency by which men are not only re-
formed but by which they are born again.

Fourth, *by this constant use of the Scripture the congregation, old and young, get enlisted in, become acquainted with, and attend to the Scriptures.* In this
day of complex civilization, when our contacts with
human agencies and occupations have become so
tangled, when so many have lost their way, no consummation is more devoutly to be wished than that our
people should be Christ-followers. That is not possible
except they become increasingly acquainted with the
Bible.

I am reminded of a conversation held with a banker
in 1931 concerning the fiduciary responsibility of some
great men in the business world and especially to that
group to which he belongs. I had said some rather
positive and caustic things about certain cases with
which I and some friends were connected, when he
suddenly turned on me a steady gaze and said, "But,
I want you also to remember, that no group of men
are more responsible for the situation than preachers.
They have ceased to proclaim the Word of God to

men and have too often turned their pulpits into plat-
forms, their sermons into talks and speeches for the
propagation of their personal opinions and theories
on things they don't know anything about. They have
lost the 'thus saith the Lord.' If they had been as
faithful for the past twenty-five years in confronting
men of this country with God as revealed in the Bible,
men would not have lost their consciences and sense
of accountability to God in their dealings with each
other." In the face of such a reply, I sat in silence.

He may be right. At any rate, he made a strong
defense for the need of a more genuine Christian
message and for the proclamation of Biblical truth.
If men do not give full honor to the Word of God
and preach it, how will we get people to honor that
Word? Let preachers preach the Word; be instant
in season, and out of season, in doing so.

To repeat, the text is that portion of the Scriptures
on which the preacher's message is founded.

1. *It may be one word*, e.g., "Repent" (Matt. 3:2).
The preacher should tell what the word means.

There are different words in a given language, Greek
or Hebrew for example, translated by one word into
English. The peacher will search if it be so in a
given instance and make it plain what is the meaning
of the word as found in the text he uses. The circumstances of the text will offer him an opportunity
to indicate its meaning to those to whom he *now* speaks,
if they would come into personal contact with the
reality of experience with God as revealed to us in
Jesus Christ.

2. *It may be a phrase*, e.g., "Who gave Himself

for our sins." He will have to indicate in the case of such a phrase what he means by sins before he can clearly indicate to just what Jesus gave Himself and what He did in such a giving of Himself.

3. *It may be a whole verse,* for example the whole of the verse just cited, when he can unfold the great purpose of God as indicated in Gal. 1:4 in sending Jesus into the world—that He might deliver us from sin and from the power of this present evil world, according to the will of God our Father—a soul-stirring prospect, in which a man can see the mercy of God in Christ Jesus. Suppose he takes John 12:32, "And I, if I be lifted up from the earth, will draw all men unto me." What confidence such a statement from the lips of Jesus betrays as to the ultimate victory of our Lord in giving Himself on the cross!

4. *It may be a paragraph or chapter* such as Rom. 8:11 or I Cor. 13:1-13, which will unfold the great concepts of Paul and the freedom and perfection of life there is in the utter acceptance of Jesus Christ, our Lord and Master.

5. *It may be a whole book,* e.g., Matthew, The Book of King Jesus, in which we have: (1) the childhood of the King; (2) the proclamation of the King; (3) the rejection of the King; and (4) the triumph of the King.

In reference to such preaching, Dr. Dale says, "I often fall on a particular verse, or a particular phrase, and show it annihilates some common error, or strengthens the evidence of some great truth, or rebukes some sin, or suggests a solemn or pathetic motive to the exercise of some Christian virtue."[6] Testimony from such a man on textual preaching ought to leave no man in doubt as to its practicality. Following such a leader will lead no man into the paths of futility. He was an efficient preacher.

What determines a man's texts for him?

First, *his constructive study carried on regularly and systematically.* At the beginning of his ministry, let the preacher commence such a study and continue it to the end of his life. *Read* all books of the Bible. *Study* the Scriptures, one book at a time. Become thoroughly acquainted with the Bible's central message, the sweep of its thought, the environment of its composition, the practical significance of its message, and its applicability in the present day and for its needs. Such a man will be amazed at the pertinence of certain great books to the present time. Of course the man who jumps about from one verse to another will not find the same values. Mere proof-text study unsupported by a consideration of the total portion of the Scripture will not discover to such as indulge themselves in it the mind of Him who inspired the writing of the Books. Probably one of the reasons for contempt that in this day falls on proof-text study, intended to support doctrines held by different groups of Christians, lies in a discovery that the portions cited are not pertinent. Texts do not mean what they seem to mean when taken out of their connections in the Scripture where they are found. Such practice in the effort to obtain a text is liable to narrow people's minds instead of broadening them. It does not give a correct knowledge of the Word of God.

Second, *events, or calendars of the church year, will give to the man who knows his Book great advantage*

in the selection of texts. In the course of twelve
months such a preacher will, systematically, bring
to the attention of his congregation the great mountain
peaks of truth found in the Christian tradition. Such
men are obligated, at specially indicated Sabbaths of
the year, to take up and present the great assets of
the Christian faith. The criticism may be justly
brought that, too often, such men are more ecclesiastical or theological than human or Biblical. But that
need not be true. Only last summer I drove around
the lake from my summer home to a little chapel of
one of the great Christian denominations, for a Sabbath-
morning service. When I took my seat I learned I
was to listen to the bishop for that section of the
country. What did he preach? He dealt with the
subject on the church's calendar for that day. If there
was anyone in that audience who went away without
some acquaintance with what the Bible taught and that
denomination believed, it was not the Bishop's fault.
He interpreted to us what the Scripture said on that
subject. We were edified and strengthened in the
Christian faith and better equipped for Christian living.
He was far wiser than the curate in charge of the
same work two or three years before, who spent his
time on a Sunday morning discussing some recent
philosophies about which no one knew much and cared
less when he had finished.

Third, *a man's text may be given to him by the
current national movements, world situations, and
events that focus in the public mind.* Current and local
events sometimes come suddenly that demand a message. If a man knows his Book, he will preach. If
he does not know his Book and make use of it, he

will only talk. The preacher may have to discard the message he has labored hard to prepare for that hour. Happy the man who, at such a time, knows where to find a text that has applicability in that hour. It is possible for a man of average intelligence and professional training to face the world in which he lives and never relate himself and his message to the needs of his times. We know some preachers do. But such men do not preach effectively. Prophets, who are the forefathers of all true preachers, were men who lifted up their voices to speak the mind of God to men on the questions that had to do with the lives of those to whom they spoke. They were men who faced their world and spoke for God to it. So ought every man. Let him, then, know what God has said in times past. He will discover the problems at the core of life in the past were very much then as they are now, and that there is a "thus saith the Lord," a revelation of His mind, and heart, and will for men that is not out of date because we have invented some machinery by which we improved our speed and lengthened our contacts.

Fourth, *the man who undertakes the development of some of the great themes of Scripture will find it cannot be done in one or even two days in the portion of time that is allotted to him.* If he has been constant and faithful in the study he will find *there are many texts that state the various aspects of the truth he wants to preach.* There are few practices more profitable to preacher and people than the development of themes in consecutive treatments. The thing he must be careful to observe in his study is to be sure he is making progress in his thinking on a given theme and that he is not going over the same thing. He must think clearly, consistently, and progressively when he undertakes "a series" on a given theme.

Fifth, then, as Dr. Herrick Johnson used to say, *texts come to him on the wing*. He urged men to cultivate the "homiletic bias," that is, the tendency to note the preaching values of life's experience and contacts. I would urge the same in respect to Scripture. Let him set the laws of association at work and learn to note the applicability of Scripture to the hour that confronts him. In his reading and study in various fields of intellectual, literary, scientific, or pleasurable reading, suggestions of homiletic value will come, which, if recorded and expanded as time and thought permit, may become of great value and usefulness in later preaching. The note-books of Phillips Brooks' college days became valuable in his Boston preaching. There is no doubt in our minds that it is in such circumstantial suggestions the voice of God's Spirit is speaking to us in what, too often, we feel, are commonplace and unimportant incidents. While we are waiting for the winds and the whirlwinds, the loud, boisterous noises, as the vehicles of the divine Presence, He goes past with gentle and lowly utterances our ears are too dull or our minds too preoccupied to hear. The truth is there is no text more timely than and so piercingly appropriate as these texts that "come on the wing," or when, as Dr. George Buttrick says, "They jump from between the lines of the book you are reading, though it may be a very secular book. They look out at you through the mirror while you are shaving. They write themselves on the wall of the house across the street. They tremble in the glow

of the evening prayer."[7]   Quite so.   And if a man
does not find use for them when they come, if he turns
them away with indifferent attention or vain excuse
for not lodging them in the best rooms of his mind,
they gradually cease to appeal for his employment
of them.

Sixth, let me mention once more *the educational
program you may have, not only for yourself but for
your people's development in Christian character, will
require and suggest many a text.*   Preaching nowadays
is too incidental and occasional in its purpose.   Men
have not conceived of their duty as pastors, with pastoral responsibilities in character building.   The man
who thinks of his responsibility for leading men to
become Christ-like will see the advantage of a constructive and coördinated course, or curriculum, for
character building.   Such a man preaches not only
to bring men to Christ, but to build them up in Christ,
to enlist them in devotion and fellowship with Christ,
and to send them out for Christ.   Such a preacher
carefully accumulates his whole preaching-instruction
material for character development.   His preaching
is so prepared and directed.   The texts for it are in-
dispensable.   They will be available if he searches
his Scripture for them and attends to the suggestions
of the Spirit of God in his reading and thinking about
them.

When the real foundations of efficient preaching are
explored and examined, we come back to this, which
must not be forgotten: The Bible is primarily the
preacher's encyclopedia of study.   He must know his
Bible.   He may dare to be ignorant about any other
book.   If circumstance or time hedge him about and

limit his range of reading and study, let him take advantage of what is available, but let him not neglect his Bible. Its history, geography, its mountain-peaks of truth, its dramatic personages, its wonderful principles for the guidance of human conduct, its teaching and instruction for awakening and clarifying faith, its inspiration to noble living, its conformation of hope, above all, its revelation of God in Jesus Christ, present preaching material with which the preacher should be familiar. The man who constantly and systematically seeks the souls of men; who would bring them to God and build them up in Christian character and who would develop his own personality, strong, vibrant, valiant, must read his Bible. He must read it for spiritual, intellectual, and cultural enrichment. He must become familiar with it for the practical use of it. In such a reading, texts will inevitably focus from it in his own mind. He will have to preach them.

CHAPTER III

WHAT TO OBSERVE IN THE USE OF TEXTS

IN THE announcement of the text to be used the following order should be observed: first, the book in which it is found; second, the chapter in which it is located; third, the verse or portion used; e.g., the Gospel according to Matthew, the eighth chapter and the thirteenth verse. This enables the hearer to fix it in his mind easily. He finds the book and locates the chapter and the verse in their proper sequences. If the preacher makes the announcement in the reverse order, anyone wishing to turn to the passage when it is announced must wait until the announcement is completed before he can start. Too often in such cases the preacher has begun to preach before the Scripture is located by the hearer. The method suggested is the most natural and correct.

The question arises when to announce the text, at the start or later, before or after the theme. There is no set time or place when the text should be announced. Often it is best to begin with the announcement of the theme of the message to be brought. Occasion or circumstances may determine not only the time but the manner. Some men do not announce the text until near the close. But this does not seem to me the best time. However, the man who always does this in the same way soon loses some measure of surprise for his audience, which is not desirable. "Variety is the spice" of good methods as well as "of life." If the preacher has an "announcer," as radio preachers have, he may include the text as well as the subject. Some examples may be given: "I wish to speak this morning on the teaching of Jesus recorded in the Gospel according to Matthew—the first chapter and the third verse." "I ask you to think with me tonight on what the author of the Epistle to the Romans says in the first chapter and the sixteenth verse." Never begin by bluntly saying, "Luke 1: 32." Address, in preaching to an audience, is just as important as in presenting yourself and your business to a man in his office. It is the talisman of personality. (Let me say, parenthetically, the same rule must be observed in the announcement of the hymns. It is incorrect and bad taste to say, "We will sing number so and so." We do not sing numbers. We sing hymns. "Let us sing hymn numbered 365," or "the one hundred ninety-first hymn." If you wish to omit a portion, indicate it by saying, "omitting the following stanzas.") We must not forget the values that always come to him who respects the good taste and the dignity of the occasion. While it may be said, "Dignity never saved anybody," nevertheless the parts of worship must be duly respected for they are worthy.

In your choice of texts usually seek the familiar ones, because in many instances they have become household words. The great basic truths of the Christian faith are found in them. In many instances they have associations that are very precious to those to whom you speak. They are in many instances challenging and arresting. They have been proved, over

and over in the history of the church to be dynamic
and powerful, playing upon the heart, engaging the
mind, and moving the will toward Christlikeness. These
familiar texts present points of contact for the preacher
with his audience that enable him to gain a ready
entrance into the citadel of man-soul.

The sermon plan is often much easier to establish
in the mind with the use of a familiar text. Of course,
the familiar text has its dangers also. It may have
been too much stressed, though this is not often so.
When a man takes the familiar texts he will be com-
pelled to give more labor to get its great values and
present them in new attractive forms, with new and
real experience and application. Familiar texts that
embody great doctrines must be used if a man is to
build strong and valiant personages for the Christian
church. Some of these familiar texts are: "This is a
faithful saying, and worthy of all acceptation, that
Christ Jesus came into the world to save sinners; of
whom I am chief" (I Tim. 1: 15). "For I know whom
I have believed, and am persuaded that he is able to
keep that which I have committed unto him against
that day" (II Tim. 1: 12). "If any man will do his
will, he shall know of the doctrine, whether it be of
God, or whether I speak of myself" (John 7: 17).
"For God so loved the world, that he gave his only
begotten Son, that whosoever believeth in him should
not perish, but have everlasting life" (John 3: 16).
"For God sent not his Son into the world to condemn
the world; but that the world through him might be
saved" (John 3: 17). "He that believeth on him is not
condemned: but he that believeth not is condemned
already, because he hath not believed in the name of

the only begotten Son of God" (John 3: 18). "And this is the condemnation, that light is come into the world, and men loved darkness rather than light, because their deeds were evil. For every one that doeth evil hateth the light, neither cometh to the light, lest his deeds should be reproved. But he that doeth the truth cometh to the light, that his deeds may be made manifest that they are wrought in God" (John 3: 19-21). "Rejoice not against me, O mine enemy: When I fall, I shall arise; when I sit in darkness, the Lord shall be a light unto me" (Mic. 7: 8). "Bring ye all the tithes into the storehouse, that there may be meat in mine house, and prove me now herewith, saith the Lord of hosts, if I will not open you the windows of *heaven*, and pour you out a blessing, that there shall not be room enough to receive it" (Mal. 3: 10). "If we confess our sins, he is faithful and just to forgive us our sins, and to cleanse us from all unrighteousness" (I John 1: 9). "Herein is love, not that we loved God, but that he loved us, and sent his Son to be the propitiation for our sins" (I John 4: 10). "O the depth of the riches both of the wisdom and knowledge of God! how unsearchable are his judgments, and his ways past finding out!" (Rom. 11: 33). "Wherefore seeing we also are compassed about with so great a cloud of witnesses, let us lay aside every weight, and the sin which doth so easily beset us, and let us run with patience the race that is set before us, looking unto Jesus the author and finisher of our faith; who for the joy that was set before him endured the cross, despising the shame, and is set down at the right hand of the throne of God" (Heb. 12: 1-2).

2. *Seek the texts that embody the great doctrines.*

This is agreeable to the office and function of the preacher. He is the ambassador for God. He is God's man in the community. Everyone expects him to be just that. Nothing is so disastrous for religion as his failure to be God's man. Certainly, it does not need to be stressed, the preacher cannot serve God and mammon or himself. He must serve God and the people in Christ's name. He must incarnate the gospel he preaches. The message of truth, the word of Revelation, the particular aspect of it you are to present and apply at a given hour, is somewhere embodied in a text or portion of Scripture. Find it and use it. Great Christians are nourished on great doctrines, which are the statements of vital truths. Be a doctrinal preacher.

This does not mean that you are to be a dogmatic preacher at any or all the time. Dogmas are statements of truth, or teachings propagated and held by a church or denomination, which all who would enter into membership with that church must accept as a condition of participation in the blessings of that church or the salvation proclaimed by it. A preacher becomes dogmatic when he insists on the acceptance of a truth or opinion as stated by himself; when he insists that any variation from this is false or heretical. But such dogmatism has often not been lacking in statements of doctrine. Sometimes it is identified in false statements of truth. Sometimes the severity of the tone or the ugliness of the preacher has been called dogmatism. Earnestness and passion have often led men to say, "The preacher is dogmatic." He may be and he may not be dogmatic. If he proclaims great doctrines he ought to be earnest, passionate, insistent. Such qualities need not prevent the grace of sweet reasonableness.

He must speak as a man who believes in the gravity of the situations for those who do not accept the truth he proclaims. There must be conviction behind his utterances. Preachers who present their message, be it doctrinal or observational, in the "take it or leave it" manner, are not efficient preachers.

3. *Be faithful to your texts.* The text must be studied in its setting and not treated as though it were given to bolster up our theme. "A man must be faithful," as Dr. George Buttrick says, "to what he finds there."[1] Discover the circumstance and atmosphere that surrounds it. Begin by asking, "Who said it? To whom was it said? Why was it said?" Undertake to understand its author by inquiring into his background, his experience, his attitude to life and human society. Study his personality revealed in the available records. Note the parallel utterances you find in other Scripture, "comparing Scripture with Scripture," and the particular circumstances to those to whom your text was addressed. Take account of all the characters that may be associated with any text taken from the Gospels and historical books. Mark the effect and purpose of their presence upon the writer in his statement and meaning of the text. Learn all you can about the place and times contemporaneous with the text.

As an illustration of what I have been saying, suppose you are dealing with words found in the Gospel according to John, the twelfth chapter and thirty-second verse. What did Jesus mean in verses 23 and 28? Evidently Jesus faced a crisis. Who said them? Jesus. Was He tempted to demit His Messiahship? What antecedent circumstances do we find? Greeks called on Philip and Andrew to see Jesus. Who were these

Greeks? Were they from Odessa or Athens? If from
Athens, did they know about the superscription—"to
an unknown God" (Acts 17:23)? Did they think that
Jesus was that God? What gave Jesus His poise and
balance, the courage of denunciation (John 12:31),
the confidence He expressed (vs. 32) in the event of
His death? Was it His acceptance of the Messiahship
(Isa. 53:1-12) with all its discipline and suffering?
The time and place and atmosphere—were they of a
schoolroom or of friendly intercourse? Was it not the
atmosphere of a struggle with enemies, with contending
armies, with deadly foes, an atmosphere of war (vs.
31)? Was it the consciousness that he would solve the
problems of sin that engaged the mind of Jesus? Was
it the conviction on Jesus' part that this was the supreme
incident in revealing God's love for men? Interrogate Jesus Himself in this fashion, "What do you mean,
Jesus, by such words—'And I, if I be lifted up from
the earth, will draw all men unto me'?" Out of such
a study and inquiry and meditation thereon the preacher
can get a message that will inform the minds, touch
the hearts, and grip the wills of men.

*Great texts are inexhaustible in meaning and as mes-
sages.* To throw new light on such texts is the way to
win the minds and hearts of men. It is much better to
win them in this way than to resort to cheap claptrap
or sensationalism. You have great precedents for such
worthy and valiant practice. Lyman Beecher, Bushnell,
Finney, Phillips Brooks, Henry Ward Beecher, Cuyler,
Jowett, George Truett, Buttrick, and a host of others
are witnesses to the opulence and power that lie in
dealing faithfully with your texts.

4. *Do not neglect any books of Scripture in your*

preaching, as some are inclined to do. Do not leave the prophetic portions to the dispensationalist; nor the apocalyptic portions to the millennialists. If some great passages or books get special emphasis in your consideration, remember the splendor of one portion is often increased by other portions, even as one great mountain-peak gets glory by being surrounded by other grand peaks. Never allow yourself to become a mere faddist. We have no warrant in the Word of God for lopsidedness in our character or preaching. We must declare the whole counsel of God and leave it to the Holy Spirit to give His own emphasis, where, and when, and as He pleaseth.

5. *Avoid sensational texts and texts that offer but little except the chance to explain them.* The opportunity for sensationalism is not as often in texts as in themes. But there are texts to be found that appeal for newspaper publicity, and those who have a flare for this, or want to get into the papers, are sorely tempted to use them. But a ministry built upon or given to sensationalism is not on a solid foundation nor engaged in a worthy evangelical practice. When considering a text marked by grandeur of expression, be not too hasty to seize upon it. Such a text may often promise too much, and your utterance will be an anticlimax, or it may arouse a criticism, and you will be unable to meet it.

In preaching there are certain great loyalties a man ought always to observe with courage and faithfulness. First, *he ought to be true to the great aim of the Christian ministry, which is to lead men to become Christlike, not only as individuals but in social relationships.* Society will be reconstructed, its institutions, manners,

and principles will express goodness, equity, and jus-
tice, only when we get reconstructed men and women.
"Except a man be born again he cannot see the kingdom of God." The aim of the true preacher is so to
labor in the proclamation of the truth that processes
of better life may be initiated, that the Spirit of truth
and life may use it to bring about the new life in
Christ. This, then, is the hope for the world. The
preacher is God's great agent in this process that means
new life for the world.

*Again, be true to your commission to preach the
gospel.* The good news is that God has come into the
world in the person of Jesus Christ. It was no other
than John Ruskin who called our attention to people's
ignorance of what Christianity really means. He was
describing his visit to the Campo Santo and what he
found there: "Briefly, the entire doctrine of Christianity, painted so that a child could understand it.
And what a child cannot understand of Christianity,
no one need try to. In these days of the religion of this
and that—briefly let us say, the religion of Stocks and
Posts—in order to say a clear word of the Campo
Santo, one must first say a firm word concerning Christianity itself. I find numbers, even of the most intelligent and amiable people, not knowing what the word
means; because they are always asking how much they
like, and never ask, what *was* the total meaning of it,
whether they like it or not.

"The total meaning was, and is, that the God who
made the earth and its creatures, took at a certain time
upon the earth, the flesh and form of man; in that
flesh sustained the pain and died the death of the
creature He had made; rose again after death into

glorious human life, and when the date of the human race is ended, will return in visible human form, and render to every man according to his work. Christianity is the belief in, and love of, God thus manifested."[2] Such is the good news which men have been commissioned to preach, which the stalwart preachers from the Apostle Paul to George Truett have preached. Preachers are ambassadors for God, witnesses to His truth—as though God did beseech men by them, in Christ's stead, to be reconciled to God. Let preachers be loyal to this commission.

Then *a man must be loyal to his people—to those to whom he speaks.* This requires him to consider their particular spiritual needs, their circumstances of poverty or wealth, their stage of Christian experience, lest he make too great demands upon them, set the standard of Christian living too high for them. He must preach to those that mourn the word of comfort wherewith we are comforted in the gospel, speak with tenderness to the wounded, bind up the broken-hearted, proclaim liberty to the captive, and the opening of prisons to those who are bound. He must not neglect to warn the sinner. Sin is a terrible, devastating, destructive, deadly fact. It is lawlessness against the kingdom of God, of which a great many "eminently respectable people" are guilty. All have sinned and come short of the glory of God. The preacher must not neglect or hesitate to warn the sinner in his evil way. But he has also the best news for him: "If we confess our sins, he is faithful and just to forgive us our sins, and to cleanse us from all unrighteousness." The preacher must be loyal to those to whom he speaks. "It is not enough," says one of our great teachers, "to tell men

Christ died because He loved them; the gospel of the death of Christ includes the fact that He died for their sins. Until man knows what sin is—sin as distinguished from mere natural defects and infirmities which they may attribute to their temperament and to the physical constitution which they may have inherited from their parents; sin as distinguished from mere vice, which conscience condemns, and which in the absence of any belief in the authority or even the existence of the living God, conscience would continue to condemn; until, I say, men know what sin is they can see no meaning in a large part of St. Paul's teaching of the death of Christ. Until they are troubled, ashamed, and alarmed by the consciousness of sin, they will listen to a large part of the gospel with a moral indifference or even with moral resentment." The preacher whose message never includes such witnessing to the curse of sin is not faithful or efficient.

Once more, a preacher must be true to himself, to what you are as well as to what *you hope to be* and are *striving to be*. In personal interviews with men about their personal relation to Christ, I have found them endeavoring to be loyal to themselves in avoiding a pretense to be something they are not. Why is it not true then and equally obligatory that a man ought to be faithful in showing his loyalty to what he is and what he hopes to be and is striving to attain? As a preacher of the gospel, let us be true to the measure of grace that has been given unto us, and to the promise of what is ahead of us. "Not as though I had already attained, either were already perfect: but I follow after, if that I may apprehend that for which also I am apprehended of Christ Jesus" (Phil. 3: 12).

We conclude by summing up the advantage of textual preaching:

1. It will express the mind of God to your people.
2. It will preserve the balance of emphasis in your preaching.
3. It will produce the most opulent returns for your study.
4. It will save you from garrulous tendencies and aimless utterances.
5. It will supply pertinent subjects for your preaching.
6. It will often readily suggest the plan of treatment for your subject.
7. It will guarantee the Scriptural development of your people.
8. It will guarantee the blessing of God on your people and preaching.

Dr. Herrick Johnson has well epitomized what we have said in a paragraph on being faithful to your text: "Fidelity to your text will secure the greatest variety in preaching, the best exegesis, the most Scriptural instruction, the best honor to the Spirit, and, hence (the conditions being in all respects the same) the most success in winning and building souls."[3]

CHAPTER IV

THE SERMON SUBJECT

FOUR words have been used to describe that part of the sermon we are now to consider. They are "title," "topic," "theme," and "subject."

Dr. Herrick Johnson contends that "theme" is the correct word, because it is particular and specific. "Subject is too broad and general to be applied to the sermon. Repentance is not the theme of a discourse which is designed to show the necessity of repentance, if one would not perish. It does not fix a boundary to the subsequent discussion. And a theme must do that if it is to tell the truth."[1] Dr. Arthur Hoyt agrees with Dr. Johnson, defending his position in a like manner. He says, "Faith is a *subject*, but 'the promptitude of faith' is a *theme*. 'Faith' is broad and general, it makes no affirmation or denial; it suggests no limits or purpose. 'The promptitude of faith' is specific, gives definite relations and has an unmistakable purpose."[2] "Subject," however, has some good sponsors for its use. Dr. David R. Breed, in his chapter on textual analysis, says, "Select so much of the given passage as will furnish a complete subject." "The text being determined, the preacher will then proceed to express his subject."[3]

58

Dr. Ozora S. Davis considers the teachings of Hoyt and Genung, as presented in his *Practical Elements of Rhetoric*, but he concludes thus: "We shall employ the word 'subject' here in the restricted sense of the 'theme' or 'topic' recognizing the distinction noted above (of Hoyt and Genung) but feeling that the current usage, sermon 'subject' is generally clear and that to substitute the word 'theme' would confuse rather than clarify the matter."[4] "The same principles obtain in reference to both title and subject."[5] Dr. Davis seems to recognize the correct word to use is theme; but because of the more frequent use of the word subject he uses it to designate the same thing as Dr. Johnson and Dr. Hoyt do in the word theme. If, therefore, we should use these words interchangeably, we should seem to have good authority for doing so. "Theme" is the technical word; "subject" the word in common use.

The qualities of a theme, or subject, must be characterized by directness in statement, being specific in thought, single in meaning, combined with comprehensiveness, including the total thought to be set forth about the text chosen. These requirements suggest the importance of the theme.

(1) *It must state definitely and precisely what the preacher has been thinking about and what he is going to talk about.* His theme sets a limit beyond which, if he is true to his theme, he will not go. Such a man will avoid the temptation into which a preacher fell. As reported by one of his audience, when asked, *"What did the preacher talk about?"* he answered, "He didn't say." Evidently, one of his audience did not know— and there were probably others who were in the same plight.

(2) *The theme must be clear in its statement*. Nothing is more important for the preacher than to be clear. He owes it to himself and to his audience to be clear in his thinking and speaking. There are too many things people cannot see through without a tax upon their attention. Of all speakers who address the public, the preacher must avoid this. He should be most careful to attain clarity in his statements. He thus recognizes the rights of his audience. They have a right to know exactly what he is talking about. Henry Ward Beecher cautioned young preachers to observe the law of "economy of attention." They cannot do so unless their theme be clear to their own minds and, so stated, it will be clear to the audience. People have little disposition to try to find out what a preacher is talking about. He must make this known to them at once. They have the right to claim this if they are expected to listen.

(3) *The theme must be intelligently stated*. It is the first indication of the preacher's style, which, as we shall consider it later, should be described by clarity, attractiveness, and force. The theme should possess these three qualities and, also, it should be brief and concise. These qualities are of great advantage to the audience and secure their attention at once. They will be able to follow such a theme. It makes a distinct and definite impression. It is awakening and challenging. A concise and intelligent statement of the theme excludes the irrelevant and unimportant factors that clutter the minds of people. It helps the preacher to secure that movement of thought which begins with information and, which, stirred by emotion, ends in a decision on the part of those to whom he speaks.

(4) *Then again, the theme should be interestingly stated.* Remember Dean Swift's remark, "Dullness in the pulpit is the sin against the Holy Ghost." Dullness is a serious offense, if not as serious as Swift declared. At any rate, dullness must be shunned. Interest on the part of the audience depends upon the preacher's escape of dullness. This will be determined by a number of factors: (1) the preacher's natural gift for interesting people and being interested in people; (2) his knowledge of their circumstances and personal interests; (3) his gift, natural and acquired, of discovering points of contact and of connecting with them; (4) his knowledge of his subject and his being able to speak of it with interest.

To be interesting is not always easy. It is not easy to state a truth with such brevity, combined with comprehensiveness, as to satisfy the demands both of the audience and the sermon. The audience have their mental limitations. They are not dull nor wanting in intellectual awareness, perhaps; but some of them are alien in feeling, remote in interest, or indifferent to such a degree the preacher finds it hard to enlist them. Too often the temptation besets him to be clever or sensational. If so, he is reminded that a man cannot be clever and reveal Christ at the same time. Nor can he be sensational and reverential toward the mysteries of truth at once. These qualities do not go together. Be earnest and sincere if you want to impress your audience with the truth. Never cease to strive to put your theme as interestingly as you can without paying tribute to the cheap and bizarre. A minister who regularly preached to audiences of from one to two thousand people, once confessed to me the state-

ment of his theme for his calendar and the press no-
tices was, for him, one of the most difficult tasks in
the week. He frequently fell into very unscriptural
and sensational ways. But this is not necessary. By
continued practice a man gains in facility in the statement of his themes and the best may be achieved.
Such a statement will seek to be timely, and pertinent to the people, to the hour and place, and to the
Scripture used as the text.

The broad rather than the particular and specific
statement characterizes the habit of many preachers.
Such men want as wide a field as is possible in which
to roam for thirty minutes. Too often they get nowhere. They leave no definite impression on the minds
of the hearers, beyond what a pleasant walk may give
to those who indulge in it. They have no destination.
They only meander about. This is of little value unless a preacher have an exceptional gift for observation of the wayside. A preacher must seek to get somewhere. He ought to have a goal, carry his audience
toward it, and get some decision at the end of the way.
He has a case to present to the court of human intelligence. He wants a verdict when the case is presented to that court. He should seek for decisions.
The statement of the theme upon which he wants that
decision must be clear and specific. If that statement
be clear and distinct and brief, he will be far on the
way, at the beginning.

How may the theme be stated? The theme may
be stated in various ways. In whatever way it is stated,
it must carry religious significance. It must indicate
its sermonic purpose; that the preacher will preach
and neither lecture, read an essay, nor give an ora-

tion. He will not engage simply in story-telling, make an argument for some philosophical position, political theory, or secular issue. The preacher expects to appeal to the conscience and to present the truth that is inherent in the Word of God. His message has to do with man's relation to God. He may be dealing with situations in human society or with a man's practices in his relation to his fellow, but when the preacher speaks, it must be clear that his position is planted squarely on the foundations of religion. Take for example this text David R. Breed cites in his discussion of the narrative sermon (Exod. 5:22-23): "And Moses returned unto the Lord, and said, Lord, wherefore hast thou so evil entreated [dealt, R.V.] this people? why is it that thou hast sent me? For since I came to Pharaoh to speak in thy name, he hath done evil to this people; neither hast thou delivered thy people at all." "This text is purely historical. There is no exhortation in it. No duty is commanded; no grace commended; no doctrine presented. How then shall the subject be presented? If the preacher announces his subject in some such terms as this, 'The complaint of Moses,' the subject, (or theme) is an historical one, and open to objection; since it relates wholly to the past. But let the subject be announced as 'Delay of Divine Deliverance,' (or Moses' controversy with the Lord) and every hearer will feel its immediate present application and force."[6]

Suppose a man proposes to discuss some definite proposition, which must not only be proved but upon which he proposes to base a plea for action. Then he must state his theme so and present his appeal to the rational intelligence of his hearers. I take, in illustration of this, a text presented by Herrick Johnson. His text is, "But grow in grace, and in the knowledge of our Lord and Savior Jesus Christ" (II Pet. 3:18). His theme is—"Growth in grace is a Christian duty." Having made a positive statement concerning grace, he must prove it. He does this under the following divisions of his sermon:

I.   Because commanded of God.
II.   Because growth is a law of all healthful life.
III. Because increase of grace is increase of power.
IV.   Because the more we grow Christlike, the more we honor Christ.

Conclusion: "Christians, you wear Christ's name, this is not an optional thing, a mere privilege to be enjoyed or not, at pleasure; well enough, and even desirable, but not vital. It is clearly as much a duty as faith is, or prayer. God's Word makes it a test of discipleship and binds it on our hearts as an imperative law."[7] The conclusion here is in the form of a direct and personal application of this theme to those who heard the sermon.

Take another on Acts 27:23-25. The theme is the spiritual leadership needed for this day (the depression years of 1929-1938). The introduction. The present economic depression is a perilous one. People lose heart, and their morale is undermined. There is a "subsidence of our national foundations." The leadership for such an hour is indicated in the character of Paul:

1. He boldly declared his consciousness of direct personal contact with God.
2. He courageously declared his allegiance to God.

3. He valiantly declared his faith in God's protecting care.

4. He steadied those who were addressed.

Conclusion: "God give us men, etc." My appeal is for men who will take such a stand, and for our citizens to follow and support such men.

Where do preachers get their themes? This is not so important as the question, has the theme got the preacher? Nevertheless, the question must be answered when asked by the student of homiletics—where do preachers get their themes?

1. We answer, *primarily from the Bible*, the Scriptures of the Old and New Testaments, the Word of God. The message of the preacher is, at its best, one given to him he is commanded to speak, he is commissioned to proclaim. It is included in the fact that God is revealed in and through Christ to man. This is the good news, the gospel: God is our Father, He loves us, forgives us, redeems us, gives His Spirit to teach, guide, and sustain us, and gives us hope of a life to come. Just in proportion to the measure in which the preacher's knowledge of the gospel is vital, that is, has become his own experience, so that he speaks as a witness of reality attested in his own life, just in that proportion will themes find him and he will speak with the authority of "thus saith the Lord." Like the Psalmist, he will be one who says, "Come and I will tell what the Lord hath done for my soul." In proportion as a man's experience broadens and deepens, continues and gains ascent, so will themes increase in plenty and pertinency.

2. Again, *occasions suggest or demand his themes.*

Events in the parish, which have gripped the attention
of his people, will present themes that cannot be denied
a hearing. The preacher must consider the religious
significance of such events and interpret the divine
mind, heart, and will as revealed to him. Men who
say, "The preacher should stick to his gospel and let
business and politics, industry and social problems
alone," mean well; but they are too often conscious
of the rebuke God has in store for their manner of
conduct in these matters for the preacher to hearken
to them. They are not touchy for the interests of Jesus.
The preacher must be. If the preacher is to be interesting, or worthy of their attention, he must interpret the gospel on the plain where men live. No
man can have a practical message who is up in the
air while his people are in the marketplace, in the
social whirl, or deafened by the clatter of the factory
and shop. People travel toward eternity on the highways of the world. The testimony of the disciples
was that their hearts burned within them when Jesus
talked with them in the way. These interests which
engage the bosom and business of men provide the environment in which the gospel must be preached. The
Bible light must be turned on that environment. The
problems and the issues they present are the sources
from which great themes arise and demand the
preacher's utterance. The paramount significance of
the incarnation of God in Jesus lies in its witness
to the fact that *God is here, on earth, as well as in
heaven.* If men were right with God here, this would
be heaven.

Not only events in the parish, but in the nation,
in the world must be dealt with and the mind of God

made known in respect to them. We pray, "Thy kingdom come, Thy will be done in earth as it is in heaven." This prayer can never be answered in a parish where the word of God's truth is not made relevant in the presentation of themes that earth suggests. Circumstances and conditions in private and public life, current practices that describe our society and civilization, the common needs of the poor, the oppressed, the sinning, and suffering, the discouraged, and brokenhearted, the sick, and the dying—from all of these are voices calling to the preacher in the name of God and humanity.

But from whatever source a theme may come to him demanding expression, the preacher must surround it with the atmosphere, the mind, and spirit of the Word of God as revealed in Christ. The preacher who gets his themes from his surroundings must be sure that he keeps close to God in speaking on them. If he fails in this he may be found to be uttering his own opinions; to be interested in the propagation of his own judgments. Not many people are interested in these. They are not concerned about the threats of the day of judgment from one of their own group. If a man speaks for God to such men and women, and his concern is for God's mind and kingdom to be established in the hearts of his people and in the world, then he may speak with positiveness and fearlessness. They know such a man speaks in love, for God is love. Cultivate a "touchiness for the interest of Jesus,"[8] then speak.

Some subjects must not be used by the preacher, some of which may have their legitimate claims for presentation elsewhere than in the pulpit.

1. *Partisan political themes should never be made the message of the preacher.* Probably many sins have been committed by preachers in the name of partisanship. I am thinking of a man who thinks of his party as the God and morality party. Whatever that party stands for in any political campaign, he is quite sure is a cause that he is warranted in mentioning in his pulpit. If he preaches upon themes suggested by party standards, he expresses the party cause or the party concept. Such men are not always found in one party. By excluding such discussions from the realm of pulpit themes we do not deprecate a man's holding to definite political convictions and to some particular party. Every man ought to have definite defensible political convictions and find his place in the party that most exactly expresses such convictions. We believe in party government; but we are not interested in, and believe it never excusable, to bring partisan politics into the pulpit.

There have been occasions when political campaigns have presented great moral issues. Moral issues are not to be excluded from the preacher's message or themes of preaching. If these are clear and definite and so manifest to the community as involving the betrayal of humanity, or the kingdom of God, they can be so easily identified with the interests of Jesus that the preacher must not withhold the Scriptures' teaching on the subject. He must appeal to men to follow the way God points out to them.

2. *Subjects of a sensational, vulgar, frivolous nature should be excluded.* I am thinking for example of a sermon theme used by an American evangelist, which he thought to have been one of the greatest in

the list of themes upon which he preached. Whatever defense he or his followers may have made for this theme of "Chickens come home to roost," it is sensational, vulgar, and frivolous in form, association, and suggestion. But it is no more so than "Microbes in the parlor," "How to break into the (denominational name) church," "Burnt pancakes," and a long list that have appeared in newspaper religious announcement columns. If a subject is worthy of treatment in a sermon, it should be introduced by proper and worthy indication.

3. *Purely scientific, historical, or critical subjects should be excluded.* They may be used as illustrative material for great and worthy subjects. Such a use may indicate their religious significance. But at the same time they are only observed in a passing reference and not as a worthy subject or treatment of a sermon. A minister was reported to the author recently as having dealt with the material developments of this country, the subject the previous Sunday being "The Government Dams-Project," without any reference to the religious idea suggested, but only the material advantage accruing to society being pointed out. This is not preaching. Neither is a man preaching when he brings into the pulpit the account of the processes and results of Biblical or historical criticism, the achievement of archeological investigation, or the historical and current philosophies. Such subjects are worthy of treatment, but they are not so for preaching. The efficient preacher does not take such for sermonic treatment. The preacher is a herald proclaiming the coming, honoring the personage of the King of kings, and the Lord of lords. He is God's

ambassador to men. God has given him His message concerning Himself, and his fellow-man; concerning His reign in the earth as well as in the heavens; concerning man's duty to God and to his fellow-man; concerning His love—that is seeking the sinner, forgiving, and redeeming, not only in time but for eternity; and it is of the fact and meaning of these great realities that the efficient preacher will discourse.

Great preachers have grandly illustrated this true concept for us. Brooks preached "The Light of the World" (John 8:12); Beecher, "What is Christ to Me?" (Col. 1:9); W. R. Inge, "Warfare, Devilish and Divine" (Eph. 6:13); H. Tydeman Chilvers, "Faith Manifest" (Ps. 48:14); George H. Morrison, "Judging for Oneself, a Christian Duty" (Luke 12:57); John Kelman, "The Garden and the Cross" (Matt. 27:59-60, John 19:41); J. D. Jones, "The Optimism of Jesus" (John 1:42); Henry Ward Beecher, "The Sure Foundations" (II Tim. 2:19); Frederick W. Robertson, "Freedom by the Truth" (John 8:32). And there are others: "A Business Man who Wanted to See Jesus" (Luke 19:2-3); "Disciples with Burning Hearts" (Luke 22:32); "Discoveries at the Supper Table," a series based on John 13:1 to 17:26.

A political, not a partisan sermon on "Administration Loyalties" could be preached on Josh. 1:16-18; another on "The Perplexity of Righteous Leaders" (Josh. 7:8); still another, "The Question of Allegiance" (Josh. 5:13).

The list of possible subjects totally in harmony with the true principles of sermon building and gospel preaching can be easily compiled, the elements of practicality and religious loyalties always observed.

Those that have been stated and used by efficient preachers in a single generation are innumerable. Where the man, called of God, with the love of Christ welling up in his own heart, crosses the crowded ways of life, sermon subjects rise up before him, while out of his Scripture will come texts and passages of record in which God has made His ways known to men. The cultivation of what Dr. Herrick Johnson called "the homiletic bias" enables the preacher to have more true subjects than occasions give opportunity to the efficient preacher to use.

CHAPTER V

THE INTRODUCTION TO THE SERMON

IN PREPARING the introduction to the sermon, one must not only think about the text and the theme, but also about those who are to hear. Let him ask, "What is the best point of contact for me to make my approach, with this theme, to this audience?" There may be times when an introduction is not needed. If there has been some external event or some situation created through which the mind of the audience has been prepared for the message, then a man can start at once on the body of the sermon. Dr. Broadus refers to two historic incidents illustrating this:

"When Cicero broke out with his opening words against Catiline, the senate was already much excited: and so with Massillon at the funeral of Louis the Great."[1] The first instance was not a sermon but an oration. But the law of rhetoric here is just the same as in the case of the sermon.

In the second instance, the introduction consisted of one sentence: "My brethren, God only is great."[2] Again, some great calamity happens destroying many lives. The community has been shocked by the disaster. In such a time, not more than a sentence recognizing the situation on which the attention of all the people is centered, is enough. These and like instances do not call for any introduction beyond the announce-

ment of a text or the utterance of a line. Again, some
outstanding citizen proves unfaithful to fiduciary responsibility or perhaps is suddenly removed by death.
Again the text itself may clearly indicate what you are
going to talk about. It then becomes not only the
text but the introduction also.

In normal conditions, however, an introduction is
necessary. Men have a natural aversion to abruptness.
When they are in their office they do not like to have
a visitor burst in upon them without being announced.
No more do they desire or expect to be suddenly assaulted by the preacher in his preaching. On the other
hand, they are pleased with a gentle approach. The
preacher must, therefore, prepare them for his message.
If they are dull and heavy, they must be awakened.
If they are cold and indifferent, they must be warmed
and won by sympathy and attraction. If they are ignorant, they must be informed. The environment of
the text, its relevancy to them and the times, its meaning, and the importance of the truth—some one or
even all of these, become the ground for an introduction to the message that is to be brought.

Of all the factors involved in efficient preaching, no
one bulks more largely in determining the introduction
than the audience itself. "There is but one real rule
to beginning a sermon," says Dr. A. J. Lyman. "Begin
where the people are."[3] This is excellent advice.
Consider the audience first, their present state of mind,
their acquired knowledge, the views they now hold,
their interest or indifference. Treat them with respect
in presenting yourself and your message. Then you
can proceed with the body of your discourse. "The
introduction has two chief objects: to interest our

hearers in the subject, and to prepare them for understanding it."[4]

When should the introduction be prepared? It may be written either before or after the sermon. "In writing a book," says Paschal, "the last thing a man finds out is how to begin." But it is not so when writing a sermon. Whenever the preacher knows what he is going to talk about and knows his people, he can prepare his introduction. Dr. Ozora Davis[5] tells us that the British orator, John Bright, "gave the greatest attention to the preparation of his introductions." Well he may have so considered, for the introduction a man has to any situation, of which he wants to become an integral part, is of first importance. As with a man, so is it with a sermon.

There are certain considerations that must be taken into account when preparing his introduction, in addition to what has already been indicated.

1. *Consider the dominant interest of those to whom you speak.* If you are to present a subject about which they do not agree with you, then they must be won over. Some thought, either unknown or unconsidered, that is of practical or vital interest, may be brought before them. The connection of your theme with some great cause or conviction may be pointed out. If your theme might be considered small, or unimportant, its rightful place in the estimate of some accepted as authorities may be set forth.

2. *Consider the intelligence or ignorance of those to whom you speak.* One has to remember the average intelligence of the American citizen is not very high, according to government reports taken in the enlistment of soldiers in the Great War. It is never safe

to presume on their ability to comprehend the abstruse
or on their acquaintance with the Scripture. Some
of the facts with which the preacher is familiar may
have been never heard of by the greater part of his
audience. If knowledge of such facts is important
as a prerequisite to an understanding of the message,
then the introduction may acquaint them with such
facts. The author once preached a sermon on the
Israelite maid in Naaman's house, to be informed at
the close that his message had failed of its purpose
because the preacher presumed upon his audience's
acquaintance with what is recorded in the Naaman
story found in II Kings 5:1-27.

"The preacher comes to the pulpit aglow with his
theme. It has been on his heart and has come to be
'a fire in his bones.' He would kindle that fire in
his hearers. But the hearer may be conditioned in
indifference and need quickening; or in ignorance and
need enlightening; or in prejudice and need conciliating. In any event the one design is the preparation of the mind of the hearer to receive the truth.
And this design will be accomplished in one or more
of these three ways: by awakening interest, by helping
to understand, by disarming prejudice."[6]

3. *Consider the hour, or timeliness, of what you
are to say.* So far as the average American audience
is concerned, they know something of the great fundamental teachings of the Gospel. But the way they
should be introduced will differ almost with every
occasion and audience. The question is, then, "How
shall I approach this audience?" Never presume that
you can with equal success approach all audiences in
the same way, with exactly the same utterance pre-

viously used with the same success. It cannot be done.
The success with which you confront your audience
and preach, on every occasion, will depend very much
upon the adaptability of your introduction to the audience and the occasion. I have preached repeatedly
on sin, on forgiveness, on prayer, using the same texts,
but no introduction has ever been used verbatim a
second time.

4. *Keep constantly in mind—the audience must be
made acquainted with your subject.* A beginner often
gets hold of a good story that grips his attention, and
he says to himself, "That will make a splendid introduction." But the question should be asked, "What
has this to do with my message? Does this express
the central thought of my message, or is it just a good
story? Is it adaptable to my people and this occasion?" Unless it does have respect to these elements
it had best be set aside. Often some interesting situation opposite to that which is to be presented presses
upon the attention of the preacher. It is possible
to conceive of such an opposite being useful in an
introduction. If the contrast is sufficiently strong in
its opposition to the statement of the theme or the
body of the sermon to appear to all, and to make
the theme and its treatment impinge on their minds,
it may be used.

5. *The character of the introduction must be in
keeping with the treatment of the subject:* with its dignity, its importance, its comprehensiveness. Never
trifle with your subject by attempts at being facetious
or dramatic. Be sober, earnest, and respectful to your
subject matter as well as to your audience. In making
an introduction of people to each other, both parties

to the introduction should feel they are being honored. So again, when introducing your subject matter for the sermon, make the introduction with a dignity that becomes it.

Some Things to be Avoided in the Introduction

1. *Avoid any apology.* Follow Disraeli's rule— "Never apologize." "An apology is never to be made,"[7] says David R. Breed. Never apologize for taking the subject you are to present. That is to create in some minds doubt as to the propriety of your chosen subject. It creates an unfavorable attitude toward your message more often than a favorable one. If you have found it difficult to decide on what subject to preach, do not mention it in your "opening remarks." Keep that to yourself. Having once prepared for the occasion, deliver what you have prepared as though no struggle had occurred in your own mind. An apology always starts a man off with a divided mind. He seldom recovers from the impairment during the rest of his utterance. He has used a "bad psychology." Never, above all things, apologize for yourself—for inadequate preparation, for the interference of conflicting claims on your attention, for physical indisposition. Some one or all three of these embarrassments may have confronted you previous to the hour of your utterance; but that is past. You are called upon to live, live in the living present, "heart within and God o'er head." Men who make such apologies are bidding for sympathy or trying to defend their conscious inadequacy for the hour that confronts them. Their inferiority complex has got the best of them. They are usually defeated before the introduction is finished.

2. *Never present any portion of your argument in the introduction,* unless your introduction is the outline of the course you expect to follow. Leave all arguments for the body of the sermon. If you do state the main headings of the discourse, do nothing more than that. Wait until you come to the treatment of each division to make the argument. Never anticipate your argument before you are ready to make it, its logical or its spiritual results. "The introduction must not embody a thought which is essential to the main discussion. This is an error of structure to which the inexperienced and impulsive writer is prone. Approaching the work of composition with a mind fired by the subject, he finds those ideas which are cardinal to its prominence in his thoughts and he can scarce refrain from parsing out some one of them the moment he begins. The consequence is that when he proceeds in earnest to deal with his proposition he will find he has anticipated essential matter. He now has only the choice between a bald repetition of his first idea, or else a leaving of his argument fragmentary. A stone which is absolutely necessary to close his arch has been already laid in the threshold."[8]

3. *Avoid obstructions to the receptivity of your audience that would arouse prejudice or close their minds.* The announcement that you are going to preach a doctrinal sermon is inadvisable. The word *"doctrine"* is taboo in this day. Yet there never was a day in the history of Christendom when "doctrine" was more needed. If they are not thus tagged, doctrines may be preached with great freedom and accepted willingly. Sermons, like automobiles, should

be "streamlined." This is to say, they should be so constructed as to avoid bluntness of impact against the great natural oppositions to their progress as well as to secure conformity to the laws of the artistic.

Opposing views are obstacles to be avoided, except it be for the purpose of a clear and fair treatment of them for the purpose of conciliating the hearer. The hearer is then given to understand that the preacher is acquainted with the opposing views, that he fully appreciates the force and weight of these views and strength of the position occupied by those who hold them. If such positions or views be stated intelligently, fairly, and cogently, the opposition may be so won over to the preacher, his listeners will become quite open to hear what such an opponent may have to say for the other side. They may surrender to him!

4. *Avoid all elaboration and redundancy in your introduction.* "Get to the point," is the demand of every audience. The absurdity of an elaborate introduction may be illustrated in this fashion. If you are to introduce two friends, you do not go into a description of the family background or recite the history of either of them before you mention their names. The elaborate and redundant introduction to a sermon would be equally out of place. It is not your message. The introduction is intended only to make the subject of your message known to those to whom the message is to be given, to make message and hearer acquainted.

What are the Qualities of a Good Introduction?

I shall name five.

1. *Brevity.* This is the opposite of elaboration and redundancy. Nothing non-essential finds a place in

a good introduction. In our day, when there is so
much haste and impatience in people's lives, they are
intolerant of preachers who cannot be concise and brief
in all that they have to say. This lets the emphasis
fall on brevity of the introduction to what you have to
give them. Dr. Dale, in his Yale lectures on preaching, quotes Browning's lines:

> *But why such long procession and display,*
> *Such turning and adjustment of the harp;*
> *And taking it upon your breast at length*
> *Only to speak dry words across its strings?*[9]

This element of brevity in the introduction will indicate the eagerness of the preacher to get the all important message itself to his hearers, and they will
unconsciously partake of his enthusiasm and eagerness
to some degree. Dr. Broadus tells the story of "an
eminent preacher, much inclined to this fault (of long
introductions) who was one day accosted by a plain
old man as follows: 'Well, you kept us so long in the
porch this morning that we hardly got into the house
at all.' "[10] This is a great mistake. People come to
be shown into the structure you have built. Do not
linger on the porch. Be brief.

   2. *The second desirable quality of an introduction
is clarity.* That is, the introduction should be free
from indistinctness. It must not be confused in statement. It must be easy to understand. The introduction to the sermon is as the seaman's binoculars
are to him as he looks out across the sea, or to the
tourist who scans the distant landscape over which he
hopes to pass. The lens must be clean, devoid of

specks and flaws in the glass, free from dust and mists that blur the scene.

3. *The introduction must be direct.* Indirection is one of the dangers that beset the preacher. This comes about because we live in a day when the indirect approach in dealing with individuals about moral and religious values is the common practice. For example, the preacher desiring to lead some person to an acceptance of Christ will begin by asking him if he is a member of the church, or if his parents were members of any church, or by some remarks on religious values commended by psychologists, hoping in due time to get around to the point of vantage of personal relationship with Jesus Christ. When he is afraid of the secularism, or the indifference or the cynicism of those to whom he speaks, the preacher is very liable to lack in directness in his introduction. There is little to be gained by indirectness. Certainly his courage and force in the message will not be increased. In many years of work with individuals it most frequently has been found best to make a direct approach. Having secured an hour for personal interview, when the hour arrives come directly to the point—"I want to talk with you about your personal relationship to Jesus Christ." Only one thing is required in the approach—that is, the preacher's sincerity. His earnestness and interest in the one to whom he speaks must be genuine. It is no less true in the character of the introduction to the sermon. It is best to be direct. Let your audience feel and know that you are after their souls for God.

4. Dr. Johnson mentions as one of the qualities of an introduction *that it be unimpassioned.* I quote

his statement: "If the preacher is aroused the audience is not. If both audience and preacher are aflame, as they may be on emergent occasions, no introduction is necessary. But an *unimpassioned* introduction need not be trite and tame, enunciating only dull, insipid commonplaces; for this is not the opposite of passion. Let freshness and vivacity and vividness keep the preacher from mere platitudes and threadbare generalities in his opening words. Simplicity (which is his major statement) is not in these. But a highly wrought introduction will promise too much for the subsequent performance. If a preacher strike twelve when he begins, there is nothing more that he can do."[11]

Some caution must be observed in respect to this emphasis on the unimpassioned, if passion is to be properly recognized as a valuable element in the preacher and his message. If his heart has been stirred and his emotion enlisted in the preparation of his sermon, let him not allow himself to become cold and distant in the preparation of his approach. Let him remember warmth, religious fervor, passion in religious utterance are of first importance. But a fire to be of any service must be under control. Heat that is not regulated and guided, that is turned on fiercely, is liable to destroy not only its conduit or conveyor but all that it is intended to improve. Let the preacher, therefore, remember heat, gradually applied, is the true way to prevent accidents or failure. Let him remember the audience must be handled carefully. His heat, therefore, however high, must be gradually applied. But let him be possessed of the heat and the power. We must remember one of the words for primitive preaching among the people of Israel was *nabi,* whose root meaning was to "boil over, or bubble up." Such a spectacle ought not to be too gentle in the introduction.

5. *Then, again, the cardinal virtue of all in the introduction is interestingness.* The introduction must be interesting. It is impossible to say just in what quality it lies or how it may be attained. The personality of the preacher, his appearance, his bearing, the tone of his voice, and the correctness and purity of his speech—all these are a great part of interestingness in the beginning as well as in the total message. If a preacher has the sympathy to feel with his audience and the judgment to appraise the "human interest" elements involved in his message, he can hardly fail to be interesting. He seizes at once on that factor in his problem and makes the most of it. Take for illustration Philip's approach to Nathanael recorded in the Gospel of John (1: 45). He seized on a common national interest set in the heart of every Jew—the hope of the Messiah's advent. Note with what vivacity he says, "We have found him of whom Moses in the law and the prophets wrote, Jesus of Nazareth, the son of Joseph." Herein were recognized the national hope expressed by the ultimate authorities in their historic leadership, and including the element of surprise at the discovery made, its reality in their immediate environment. To mention its seeming unlikelihood, expressed by Nathanael, was a most interesting introduction to John's account of the sequence.

In closing this subject of the introduction to the sermon, let me give two illustrations from contemporary preachers. The first is from "Seeing the Invisible," by the Rev. Harold Cooke Phillips. His subject is "The

Prince of Peace"[12] (Matt. 5:21-22). "We have heard that it was said by them of old—but I say unto you." "We shall speak today of the wisdom of Jesus as it bears on what is considered the greatest social problem of our age—the problem of war. It is unnecessary to speak of the steps which we have taken—on paper—to abolish war. Suffice it to say that what has been written on paper remains to be written on our hearts. No marching works without power. Peace needs and must have a motive—a motive that is moral. It is in behalf of this necessity that we speak.

"There are many ethically-minded people today who wonder why it is that when we talk of peace we should talk of Christ. The causes of war, they tell us, are quite evident. They are largely economic. The problem of war, we are assured, is thus a human problem. Why should we befuddle an ethical issue by bringing in religious considerations? While such a statement no doubt contains much of truth, it rather betrays only a partial understanding of the problem. Every great social problem is ultimately a moral one. You cannot change the gear of human life from war to peace by throwing out the clutch. The shift is not mechanical, but moral. It demands adjustments that are deep seated. If, therefore, we insist today that Christ has a tremendous contribution to make to the world's peace, it is because He has touched life at its deepest sources. One is not belittling the baffling problems which will tax those technically capable of solving them, when one insists that the basic problem is a moral one. It is because Christ illumines this problem that He stands in the vanguard of the peace movement. Let me, therefore, mention in no sense exhaustively a few of the contributions which Christ by His life and teaching makes to peace."

Then follows the sermon with these contributions Jesus made to peace:

    I. Faith that peace is possible.

    II. The utter futility of force.

    III. His concept of brotherhood, implicit in His teaching of the kingdom of God.

This sermon has about thirty-three hundred words in it, approximately one-tenth of them in the introduction. It clears away objections. It gives a reason for presenting Christ in dealing with an ethical and social problem. It launches the sermon at once into the discussion.

Take a second from *The University of Experience*[13] entitled "Teachers and Disciples." This sermon from which the introduction is taken is by Dr. Lynn Harold Hough. His text is Matt. 11:1: "His disciples came unto Him." "The relation of teacher and disciples is one of the most venerable and one of the most distinguished of the experiences which have fallen to the lot of the children of men. When the teacher has arrived, civilization has begun to lift up its head. When the disciple has arrived, brilliant flashes of intellectual insight have begun to be transformed into continuity of mental life. The world has begun to be capable of an intellectual tradition."

This introduction has seventy-six words for a sermon of approximately a total of thirty-five hundred words. Then Socrates, Plato, Aristotle, Abelard, Thomas, and Christ, whose disciples came unto them, are presented.

Something that belonged to and was peculiarly each teacher's mind and method are suggested. Personality traits are then indicated, which give Christ the highest and most unique place as the supreme Teacher of men. These introductions will be found to include all the excellencies and requirements of what we call efficient preaching.

Acts 13:38:: 39 –

to know what good things we have by the coming of Christ, and what we are to hope for at his hands.

"Be it known to you" – nothing should hinder them from knowing such an excellent and plain matter, it was absurd that those benfi of God should be hidden from the faithful which were offered by Christ.

Col 2:13. – we are all enemies to God through sins

"And from all things" the Jews ceremonies were to led them to Christ – not Christ take the place of the ceremonies.

Act 13 38: 39

1. Preaching by man
2. Preaching for ...
3. Justification by faith
4. Not justified by laws of
Moses
5. Known by the resurrection
6. Forgiveness through Christ
7. Those that believe in for-
given.

CHAPTER VI

THE SERMON

THAT portion of the preacher's utterance to which
we now give attention has been spoken of as *"the message," "the discourse," "the argument," "the discussion," "the sermon body."* It is the all important part
of what the preacher has to say.

The body of the sermon takes various forms, depending upon the subject treated. Suppose the subject
is *The Christian Doctrine of Immortality*. In the mind
of the preacher it may be stated this way: "The Christian doctrine of immortality teaches that men and
women who live lives of faith never die." His treatment of the subject will then take the form of an
argument to establish the proposition. The divisions
of his sermon will be arranged so as to prove the proposition laid down in the theme.

If his subject be the statement of a fact, his sermon
will present the various points of meaning of such a
fact for those to whom he speaks. The preacher makes
no effort to establish the fact. He assumes that is already
accomplished. He proceeds, therefore, to indicate how
important this fact is for those to whom he speaks.
He may not do this directly but, having stated his
observations, he may leave it to his audience to make
the inferences as to their universality and pertinency,

e.g., "There was a man named Zacchaeus . . . and he sought to see Jesus" (Luke 19: 2-3). The theme is *A man who wished to see Jesus.* The preacher then proceeds to state the facts he finds in this record and what happened when Zacchaeus saw Jesus.

The preacher may make a series of observations on certain chapters such as John 13:1—17:26. From data found in said chapters, he declares, "Jesus expected His death on the cross." His sermon will, then, as in the first instance stated, be a series of proofs taken from the evidence found in these chapters. The proofs may be arranged according to their order as found in the progressive account recorded from chapters thirteen to seventeen. Or he may give them a rhetorical arrangement in which the movement is an ascending series of proofs.

Again the preacher may imagine himself in the position of a stranger to the Gospels, reading them for the first time. He observes this is a record of what happened at the Last Supper. He sets down his separate observations under the heading, *Discoveries made at the supper table of our Lord.* He particularly sets down items descriptive of our Lord's relation to His disciples. These would be something like the following: 1. Jesus' concern for their attitude toward life (John 13:1-17). 2. His concern for their attitude toward Himself (John 13: 18-30). 3. His concern for their attitude toward each other (John 13:31-35). 4. His concern for their peace of mind about the future (John 14:1-15). 5. His concern for their loneliness and for companionship (John 14: 16-31). 6. His concern for their being useful and productive (John 15: 1-11). 7. His abiding love for them (John 15:12-19). 8. His concern for their correct view of life's experience (John 15: 20-27). 9. He assures them that God has not deserted them (John 16: 1-9); and so on to the end of that last evening together. He may select any number of such observations that the time allotted will permit him to speak upon. With appropriate indication of their practicality in the lives of those to whom he speaks, his sermon is made. The number of these items should usually not be more than three or four. Sufficient comprehensiveness may be attained in that number. That number may, when clearly and definitely stated, be easily remembered. The smaller the number of divisions, the more likely will he secure a wider appeal.

Different factors are involved that help to determine the particular type of sermon and the method employed. The circumstance and occasion calling forth the sermon indicate certain lines of treatment to be followed. The purpose to be accomplished, the character of the audience, and other elements make certain demands of the preacher who wishes to be efficient that are inescapable. The sermon is like a building. It has a particular purpose to serve. There are certain objectives to be reached. These demand definite combinations of materials. The preacher is both architect and builder. They demand also certain plans and specifications that the architect has to take into account and which the builder must follow. The preacher who thinks of his "prize" sermon as suitable for *every* occasion, time, and place, is sure to be booked for a rude awakening.

But the preacher is fortunate in the fact that *the text chosen or suggested often presents a plan for its development*—at least its necessary outline or main divisions. Suppose the text is a short, pregnant portion

of Scripture, such as Rom. 1: 16-17. The points of
emphasis are clear. The subject is indisputable. In such
a case, the plan is readily determined. The theme is
The Apostle's pride in the gospel. The sermon outline
is, clearly, a statement of three reasons for this pride.
I. *Because the gospel's purpose is to save men.* II. *Because the gospel is universally effectual.* III. *Because
the gospel reveals God's righteousness.*

The Apostle declares one thing about the gospel in
this short passage that may also become the theme
of a sermon, i.e., *The power of God*—"It is the power
of God," etc. Such a topic offers and demands the
preacher's best effort. He may, therefore, speak of
the power of God exhibited: I. *In the person of Christ.*
II. *In the gospel He brought.* III. *In its accomplishments in human experience.* If he choose a lengthy passage of Scripture, as, for instance, one of the Epistles
for exposition, the plan may not appear so explicit.
The preacher must search for the central theme of the
Epistle and state it clearly. Then he will mark the sub-
divisions of this theme as presented in the Epistle and
these will supply him with the principal divisions of
his sermon plan. He may find his sermon takes the
form of an argument in which he supports the theme
he has announced as the subject of the Epistle. Whether
the logical or the rhetorical demands will determine the
order of the major divisions of his sermon will be
determined largely by the preacher's personality or
the attitude of his audience.

In selecting a long passage from the Gospels, such as
was suggested, he may state his subject in forensic
form or some other form. If in *forensic* form, then he
may find the matter of his argument in that particular

passage or he may cover the whole range of Scriptural teaching. It is only required that the divisions of his sermon plan be manifestly essential parts of his theme, and his theme manifestly found in the Epistle. When he selects a series of facts for observation it is only required that they have *a single thread of thought binding them together* as coequal parts of the subject chosen and stated as the theme of the discourse. The facts chosen for presentation at a particular time will be determined by the preacher's immediate purpose, by the circumstance and occasion to be served, by what he plans for, educationally, in the future.

But in every event the preacher must think and plan methodically. Whatever style of treatment he may decide to give his theme, he must indicate clearly. This lends strength and charm and force to his utterance. It is the nature of efficient preaching that it exhibits a plan. There must be a starting-point and an end. These two cannot be avoided. Between these two the course should be straight and clearly charted. It is the only ground of assurance to your audience that you are going to get to a desired haven. To drive like Jehu without knowing where one is going is to court futility and wrecking. But it is seldom desirable to announce your plan. To do so at the beginning of your message is to betray your sequel. When the plan is announced too much may be anticipated. The element of surprise is compromised, if not lost. It is best clearly to state each point as you come to it.

The number of divisions a sermon plan should include is often a subject of discussion. Of course the theme or the text has most to do in determining this. It will depend upon the magnitude of the thought to be presented or the audience to be addressed or the object to be gained.

1. *Be as plain and simple as possible is a good rule to follow. Have no more divisions than are needed to unfold the subject announced.*

2. *There should be as many divisions as are needed adequately to unfold your subject and present its essential parts in due proportion.* The man who states his theme clearly, briefly, and interestingly has a great advantage in working out his plan. Such a statement of the theme points your thought and reduces the number of divisions called for. This secures simplicity of treatment, contrary to the notion most beginners entertain. They seek "a broad subject" because they think it is easier to say something worth while on such a theme. But it is not so. Narrow your subject, and you will have more to say and not be required to elaborate your plan.

3. *The audience you address must be considered;* their intelligence and knowledge of what you are talking about. Let each point be as direct and freshly put as your ability will permit. Avoid hackneyed and threadbare words and phrases. Endeavor to say what you say in the language and in view of the understanding and atmosphere of those to whom you speak.

4. *The time at your disposal must always be taken into account;* in building your sermon plan as well as the material to be incorporated in the message. It is important to remember in preparing to preach that your sermon is a constituent part of a program, or "order of worship." In this order of worship, traditionally, the sermon has been given ample place; but it has become less ample in these later years. Protes-

tantism has tended strongly toward ritualism. Anthems and antiphonals, both in music and responsive readings, have grown more popular. In proportion to the place they have been given in the service, the time allotted for the sermon has been shortened. Moreover, a strong prejudice has developed against the sermon extending beyond twenty-five to thirty minutes. The man who takes the time allotted to him must be interesting to keep the attention of his audience for that time. Moreover, the attention must be caught at once if it is to be held for ten minutes! To hold it for thirty minutes is an achievement involving many factors, no one of which is more important than the consciousness of the listener that something of value is being given to him and that he is progressing—going forward to a "desired haven." If the first division of the sermon has not gripped the attention, it makes little difference what the second, third, or fourth are. The listener must be made to feel he is going forward and toward a completed message. This means both plan and material have been well selected for the purpose in view.

For public speech instruction, preachers should attend to radio requirements. Radio preachers must know precisely what they want to say and say it within definite time limits. They must pronounce their words correctly, distribute the accents properly, enunciate distinctly, and direct the voice accurately. Garrulous expansion must not be indulged. The audience must be impressed that a message practical and consequential is being uttered. Such improvements are greatly needed in all preaching. Listening to the radio preaching of any one of a half dozen men regularly on the air leads to this in the listening preacher's life and practice.

5. *The sermon plan should always be determined by the audience*; their education, preparation, and disposition toward the truth to be presented. Men whose vocation calls them to be out-of-doors in wind and weather will find it less easy to concentrate their attention than those who sit at a desk and carry on the work of administration. Farmers, mechanics, office men, *et al,* have their various conditioning experiences which the preacher must keep in mind and to which he must adjust his message. Beecher's great principle of "economy of attention" must be respected both in planning and preaching your sermon.

Of all public speakers, the importance of a plan is most urgent to the preacher. He must be bound for some definite objective. He is not as one who goes out for a morning stroll in the woods or fields, heading toward no destination. Such excursions are denied him when preaching unless he be exceptionally gifted in observing and appreciating wayside flowers and fruits and in describing landscapes. There are not many such men. Such a method as this figure suggests leads to garrulous and inconsequential talk. Therefore, avoid it. Adopt the purpose to plan your work and prepare yourself for effective expression of the message God has given you. However the subject may be treated, the sermon should have a definite plan, with its outline clear, distinct, and progressive in the mind of the preacher. The importance of such a plan may be indicated as follows:

1. *This makes the sermon intelligible.* It indicates the subject is of such importance as to engage the

Zakka

number
remember
stumble
reign
learned
holy
pursued
work

attention and the rational faculties of the preacher and
his hearers. It has mental, moral, and spiritual values.
It bears down upon the practical life and suggests
courses of conduct to which the wise may conform in
their daily thought and action. It indicates life is not a
mean and groveling thing. This is expressed in the
subject chosen. It is something noble and exalted to
which men may aspire to attain.

2. *A true sermon plan makes the sermon attractive.*
By such a plan the grace, strength, and stability of a
true architectonic product, a worthy structure, rises
before the mind. It merits praise, and the attention
and judgment of those for whom it has been built. Just
in proportion as the plan expresses the laws of form
and strength and the work of the constructive imagination, by so much will the work when completed be likely
to attract and enlist those who behold it.

3. *An accurate and consistent plan gains in per-
suasiveness.* The laws of the mind demand order and
beauty in all structures; and in processes of thought
men are led to hear and approve him who honors the
inherent demand for orderliness and completeness. To
change the figure: when they are conducted through an
unknown land, men increase in confidence, respect, and
approval of the preacher, who, evidently, has carefully
surveyed his way before he invited others to follow
him.

4. A good sermon plan, says Dr. Hoyt, *"helps the
preacher's style; gives intentness and eagerness to
speech; constructive power is gained."*[1] In the *Journal
of Gamaliel Bradford*, we have a glimpse of the method
a great biographer and lecturer followed in the preparation he made for lecture engagements. This is helpful

to those who are seeking the best methods for the presentation of their message to the public. "Always beforehand," says Bradford, "I planned out the general movement of the talk in more or less detail, dividing it into headings, in the way that seemed to me most likely to give effects of contrast and climax and especially allotted to each heading just the limit of time it seemed to me to deserve. I will not say that I always stuck absolutely to those time limits. But in the main I did it very closely and it is to that careful thinking out and systematic arrangement that I attribute most of the success these lectures had. That discipline of careful thinking out and preparation has been of immense value to me."[2] The importance of style, of which Bradford was a master, will be presented later. In this selection we have recorded here, he witnesses in support of the testimony of Dr. Hoyt. Careful construction and use of a plan contributes to effective speaking as much as to effective writing, whether of lectures or sermons. Intentness and eagerness are elements of vibrancy which lend interest to every listener and which some people do not have but long to possess. In Bradford's statement of his method, we have something of the secret by which these are gained. Not only order and beauty, but movement also—the consciousness of progress, of going forward, comes to a man who carefully constructs his sermon plan.

5. *A good sermon plan gives force and directness to utterance.* The preacher is required to concentrate his attention to make a plan. He has to initiate the process, so to speak, of assembling the powers of mind and heart and will in himself he hopes afterward to accomplish in his audience. Concentration and movement can

never be accomplished in an audience unless they are first found in a sermon, and if in the sermon, they must be in the preacher's mind who produced the sermon. If we are to have definite types of life and conviction in morals and religion, we must first of all have it in the preacher. There must be the tang of holy living if the church is to become a power in the world. These have often failed to be found in the people because there were too many preachers who lived worldly lives, who were trifling with their time and study. Being too ready to accept committee appointments and luncheon engagements, and social activities, they allowed the precious hours for study and meditation and prayer to pass. When the hour for utterance arrived, they had nothing to say. They were going nowhere so much as to luncheon clubs and committee meetings, and these were of no interest to the audience they faced. Having been nowhere, having charted no great adventures of faith and life, they could not conduct others to such a goal. Efficient preaching depends upon certain great things, one of which is boring down to hard work in the construction of an orderly mind from which may come orderly sermons.

The problem is—How is a sermon plan developed? A sermon is the result of three definite steps. First, the collection of materials of which it is to be built. Second, meditation, digestion, assimilation of the material gathered in reading and research. A man must make this material his own. He cannot become able and effectual in the use of material gathered except in proportion to the measure of its transformation and embodiment in himself. He gains strength, not simply in getting food, but in digesting and assimilating it.

Third, he must use the material in the formation of the message. Now that you have decided on your text, begin to interrogate it. What does this text say? Who said it? To whom did he say it? What was his purpose in saying it? What historical connections has it? What analogous situations does it recall in Scripture or in history? What has it to do with my purpose in preparing this sermon—does it warrant my subject and support my present attitude? Does it find me? What have the best commentators to say about it? From such a process will come material you set down for meditation upon it. You will find portions to be immediately useful and some to be set aside because they are not pertinent to your purpose.

Recall your reading on this subject or on general topics and see what can be brought from the treasury of memory that seems to bear on your present purpose: history, literature, poetry, fiction, philosophy, conversations, stories heard—select from all or any of these that memory supplies, and set them down in materials to be scrutinized for use in the sermon you want to preach.

Begin now to meditate, to brew your thought on this material. Carefully set down your thoughts and the suggestions that come to you. Develop each separate thought that seems to be of primary importance to your thinking on your subject. When you have carried this process forward to the point where you have reached some definite convictions in yourself, begin to select what seems immediately essential to an adequate presentation of the theme. Test these separate conclusions as to their essential relation to the theme and the purpose you have in mind to accomplish and as to their relation to the Christian faith, which you represent, and their consistence with the teaching of the Word of God.

Finally, arrange these thoughts and the material that you carefully select in support of them in accordance with what you deem their logical or rhetorical importance, to secure the conviction and persuasion of those who hear you preach. Always keep in mind that the preacher's business is to proclaim, to witness to the gospel, not to prop it up, but to declare it, in the purpose to persuade men to become more Christ-like.

In such a method of procedure you will discover a definite plan has emerged in the process and a sermon is already in your head and heart demanding utterance.

It is desirable now that you put it on paper—that your sermon be written. "Reading makes a full man, writing an exact man, speaking a ready man," so went the old saying. True. No man can become his best without all three. When he has gathered his material, brooded over it, and finds his plan of treatment is growing into definite orderliness of presentation, then let the preacher take up pen and paper and express his message in black and white.

The student may feel this is a demand of attention in the steps of procedure that kills the spontaneity of the spirit in the preparation and delivery of the message. He may say this is too mechanical. If he does think or feel so, let him remember that in due time these steps will become "second nature" to him and the freedom of the spirit will be released in lines of habit that are intelligently set for the attainment of the right ends. It may be concluded that the early years of his preaching will be embarrassed by the mechanics of preparation. It is frequently true that in our earlier years we may seem "academic." This, too, will pass, as we enrich our minds and hearts in the materials from which great preaching is possible. The gain of experience and the development of our personality are prerequisite to great preaching. Great suffering may descend upon us before we can preach effectively. Never mind. All things work together for good, if we gain experience in the right way, maintain the right attitudes, and gain the gift for expression of the truth God gives us.

CHAPTER VII

THE CONCLUSION

DR. HERRICK JOHNSON calls "the conclusion," "the *second* (the introduction being the first) minor part of the sermon." He does not mean it is unimportant. On the contrary, he says, "It is measurably decisive of the final effect. Its *verbal form* may be the product of the instant of delivery. But its *subject matter* is too vital to be given no heed until the hour strikes."[1] In the conclusion, the preacher brings his mind to bear on the problem of getting a decision on the subject matter he has presented. It is not only that you are coming to the close of your speaking; but you now are to endeavor to secure a verdict on what you have said, on the case as you have presented it. What you want, the purpose you have in presenting the message, is to get a decision on the part of your hearer. That time has now arrived. It must therefore express the depths and conviction of the preacher. It must describe the urgency and passion, the tenderness and desire you have for those to whom you have spoken. Peroration should, therefore, crown, as well as complete the sermon."[2]

It is evident then, that the conclusion must not introduce *new* matter, *new* arguments, *new* additional propositions. A conclusion may be a summary of your main arguments, upon which you now make a plea for their acceptance, and for their adoption and practice in the lives of those to whom the sermon is addressed. The wooing note will prevail in the preacher's voice and utterance. He may ask, why will his hearers maintain their previous course and join with it a plea for acceptance of the way he has presented. All that was weak or wrong in the opposing claims indicated, acceptance of the better way, already made plain, should be urged. If the truth has been presented and acknowledgment of it given, why not accept and follow it? Says Dr. Breed, "It is not the discussion of a theme in an intellectual fashion, however sacred or solemn the theme may be, which results in preaching, but the personal application of the truth of God. Therefore, the one consideration which must claim our particular attention relative to the conclusion is the very purpose of preaching."[3] We must win a verdict, or endeavor to win it, if we may be said to preach, and this is what we do in a proper conclusion.

In so far as possible it should be brief. Long, drawn-out conclusions in the shape of exhortations become ineffective in direct ratio to their length and repetition. Particularly so, if they lack in earnestness and intensity. When a man indicates lack of these two qualities in his conclusion, then his whole case may be tiresome and ineffective.

This passion and earnestness must have the evangelical character, too, for a preacher is pleading for the acceptance of good news. The preacher's personality must grow with the worth and value of what he believes is indisputably true and right for those to whom he speaks. If he has presented what he believes to be eternally true for those to whom he speaks, and without the acceptance of which life will be lost in its greatest and best significance, he will so plead. The preacher is to be pitied (and his audience, too) who does not have the burning heart.

It is clear, therefore, that the object you had in view from the beginning must now be realized. All that you have said before was leading up to what you are saying in the conclusion. If that object was in your mind and heart as you proclaimed the matter in the body of your sermon, you will have earnestness and passion in the conclusion. You had one great general purpose in your preaching—it was to make men and women Christ-like. Now you are trying for some particular aspect of that total purpose or achievement in a particular way.

The best appeal is sometimes found in a story or incident. It embodies what you have said and emphasizes its imperative truthfulness in tender and moving forms. Use it and conclude, leaving the result with God and your listener.

If you appeal to the emotions and play upon them, remember it is not simply to arouse the emotions but to enlist them in moving the intelligence and the will. It is not for the sake of the feelings that you plead. It is for conviction and action, the enlistment of the whole personality, for which you labor.

CHAPTER VIII

ESSENTIAL HOMILETIC QUALITIES OF A GOOD SERMON

THE essential qualities of a good sermon give it vitality and power. The grace, beauty, and effectiveness of a sermon are determined by its conformity to principles of sermon construction. Johnson, Lyman, Hoyt, Burrell, Broadus, Dale, Vinet, and many others emphasize the importance of these principles, which the builder of sermons should strive to observe.

Three such principles we shall mention. The first is *unity*. Unity may be defined as singleness. This is not sameness, which is a quality of substance. It expresses the quality of agreement in the matter of the sermon. Unity is one out of many. Unity tends to simplicity in contrast with complexity, oneness in contrast with multiplicity, uniqueness in contrast with diversity. Unity will lend directness, definiteness, the plain and uninvolved in contrast to the involved and confusing.

Unity calls for the concentration of the mind on a definite object. The purpose is something as it is in the case of the man who chooses a rifle with a single ball in the cartridge instead of a shotgun with its handful of buckshot in the magazine of the gun. The man who seeks unity in his sermon seeks to escape scattering his charge, as will always happen when a man uses a shotgun to bring down his game.

In unity there is something of cohesion, harmonization, and agreement in thought. Things adhere to each other. The man who seeks unity in his sermon escapes inadvertence. The unimportant and secondary, he avoids. He who seeks unity seeks to bring *one* thing to the attention of those to whom he speaks.

However important a number of thoughts may be, they are left out. They would divert the attention. They would dissipate the emotions. They would divide the mind, subvert the will, and defeat the end the speaker has in view. The speaker, therefore, puts such thoughts aside. He may not discount the importance of what he puts aside. He will find that useful on another occasion and for another subject. But now that must be left out because it lacks that directness which unity requires.

This will be particularly so in respect to illustrations. A story may be good, on first appearance too good to be missed! But unless it bears directly on the goal the speaker has set before him, it will destroy this essential unity of thought he has determined to present and on which he wants a verdict. Again, a poem comes to mind. But when its essential purpose and message is examined they are found to divert the attention. The poem would concentrate the mind on a different objective; therefore it must be omitted. He may find a choice sentence from some prose writing that seems to fit; but when introduced into the body of his discourse, he finds it does not "click," so he puts it away. To the beginner, the use of such material is a subtle temptation to depart from unity. He must say "no," however distressing or difficult it may be to do it.

All that finds us in the natural order of God's world

is described by this quality of unity. When a man goes out into the woods or fields for rest and recreation there comes to him a sense of harmony and order, of peace and quietness, a healing ministry to his disordered soul.

Often on a summer's day, just at the hour of sunset, on the bosom of a lake, after the day's work with rod and line, we have sat in our boat motoring back to the cottage in the west, and looked at the setting sun, its rays of light touching the high clouds with gold, giving glory to the whole scene. The sound of traffic far away is hushed across the water. The sense of peace and rest, of strength and hope, come anew, and make us feel how wonderful and glorious is this world that God has made for man to dwell in. How harmonious and quieting and convincing the God of the world seems to us on such a day! How glorious to live and serve in such a world! It is one world, God's world. Faith and hope and love unite to make us strong. Gladness and strength return. And when we push in to the shore, wearied with the engagements of the day, we are, nevertheless, above all, at peace with ourselves and with Him who made this harmonious place. There is no confusion in this world.

But there, we learned, also, the same lesson in the storm. Black clouds gathered on the horizon. Like an organized host of valiant men, they came on and on until their courageous breath cooled our hot faces. They were moving in perfect order. Closer and closer they came. On the surface of the lake little riffles in perfect union began to advance before them. Then, as the heavy troop of clouds moved up, these riffles were lashed into great waves that seemed to draw from the very depths of the lake, rising up as if to join the valiant clouds. The tops of the trees now bent with the winds that moved resistlessly upon them. Nothing loose or unanchored could stand before them. Those winds were not divided. They were not at war with themselves. They were a unit. They swept all before them.

So it is with men. The greatest compliment I have ever heard paid to a man was uttered by a young woman who described that man, fast approaching seventy. She said, "He is the best unified personality it has been my privilege to know." How often this is expressed in the New Testament. "I and my Father are one." "I came not to do my own will but the will of Him who sent me." "Holy Father, keep through thine own name those whom thou hast given me, that they may be one, as we are." This is the singer's vision for the church:

> *We are not divided,*
> *All one body we.*

This is unity, not uniformity; unity in variety. This is the law of life, and it is the first law of convincing thought. It is also, the first law of the sermon. Every preacher should seek to gain it in his building of his sermon.

How may unity be secured?

1. *Be sure that what follows has essential elements of that which has gone before.* When the theme is stated, each division of your sermon must lie within the theme. The more evident this is to those addressed, the greater its effect in conviction and persuasion. Not only so—it contributes to the sense of progress in the treatment of the theme. So with every part of each particular division. Be sure what follows grows

out of or is an essential element of the subject under consideration.

2. *Each paragraph should be a unit, distinct and separate, but as one of several links in a chain.* Like the chain, also, remember, the strength of the chain is determined not by the number of links but by the weakest link. Endeavor to make each paragraph a thorough and complete treatment of the subject of that paragraph. Never allow a second consideration to creep in. That leads to confusion, weakness, and disorder.

3. *Each paragraph must be linked to that which has gone before and which follows after.* Correlation of thought maintained by correlated paragraphs unfolds the theme step by step and gives not only strength to the sermon but brings pleasure to the hearer. No confusion disturbs his mind. He sees the unfolding of a canvass every figure of which is clear and distinct and which, combined, complete the total concept when the work of unfolding is complete.

4. *There is no overlapping in such a piece.* Things are not tacked on nor dragged in to fill up space and take time. There is no repetition that bores and fatigues. Listeners are kept awake and alert to catch each note of this harmonious symphony of thought and speech.

5. *Let each paragraph be positive.* Omit "if" and "perhaps." Of course there are times and places where these words are necessary and cannot be omitted. But when they introduce elements of uncertainty, doubt, or as "states of mind still contingent and dependent," avoid them. They represent secondary and additional, subjoined and subordinate elements that blunt the drive and force of utterance. Speakers who hold the atten-

tion and move the will deal with certainties and not contingencies.

6. *Unity is attained with the use of the simple rather than the complex sentence.* The ornate and grand in oratory has been identified with the long sentence, with many and lofty words, multiplied and grandiloquent clauses, picturesque and beautiful phrases. But this kind of speech is out of fashion. The simple and direct sentence is demanded. Oratory may suffer; but attention is commanded, secured, and held with the use of the short and simple forms of speech in this day.

The second essential element of a good sermon is *order in the arrangement of its material.* Whatever your theme, the materials with which you develop it have a proper sequence to be maintained. Students beginning to preach are often liable to put their most effective material in the introduction. They do this because this material is so obviously germane to the theme. They cannot await the opportunity to use it where it will be most effective. This happened only yesterday. The novice was to preach his senior sermon on "The Friend of God." He wanted to make the distinction between a friend and a servant. Out of his own experience he had stated the case. He had done it well. This he made his introduction. Not another single thing he said in the body of the sermon was so vital to the purpose he had in mind in preaching the sermon. But this valuable matter was out of place and was liable to be forgotten entirely by his audience before he had gone far in the utterance of his message. His utterance was an anti-climax. It had to be re-arranged.

1. *Arguments should be arranged according to their*

nature. There are two great divisions of arguments. They are either *a fortiori* or *a posteriori*. We quote from Dr. John Broadus, "Arguments *a priori* generally precede others as they prepare the mind more readily to receive the *a posteriori* proofs. Thus, after presenting the *a priori* probability that a revelation would be given to man, and further, that such a revelation would be accomplished by miracles, we may gain a hearing for the testimony that miracles have been wrought and in connection with them that a revelation has been given. Here the testimony falls in with an antecedent probability. But if we first bring forward the testimony that miracles have taken place as insulated occurrences, without any known or conceivable purpose, it has to encounter a powerful antecedent probability against miracles."[1]

2. *Arrange your arguments according to their relative importance.* The less important should come first so that the convincing, persuasive power of your utterance may be in an ascending scale. This order is not determined, primarily, by the view of the preacher, but the estimate of the hearer. A man must always have regard to his audience. The *audience* is to be moved to action. The preacher has been already moved. If the audience is moved it probably will not be by the same order of arguments that moved the preacher. If the attitude of the audience is unfriendly to the subject, that order of arrangement which is conciliating and enlisting must be recognized and followed in dealing with them. Their information and initial state of mind must be taken into account. He will then introduce and briefly present what they will recognize as important, and attain his purpose to lead them forward to

conclusions they have not previously reached. If they are already informed and in agreement with the preacher up to a certain point, he may present only such new arguments as he may think calculated to move them to *act* in accordance with his purpose.

There are two interesting exceptions to this general practice among successful preachers that come to mind. The first is Phillips Brooks, who, his biographer says, usually put his strongest argument first. The second is Dwight L. Moody, a great admirer of Brooks, and possibly a student of his method, who insisted on putting his strongest argument first.[2] It was in accordance with his nature and probably best for him. He assaulted his hearers at once with his strongest argument. Great and successful as Brooks was as a preacher to his congregation, and as Moody was in evangelistic preaching, it would be a doubtful procedure for other men to follow their method in arranging their material for persuasion.

3. *All your material, historical references, illustrations, supporting authorities, poetry, quotations, constructive thoughts, arrange according to their pertinence and appositeness to the theme and purpose you wish to accomplish.* There is a place for everything. Certainly everything ought to be in its place. This secures movement and power in the impact of your utterance to the audience. Since there is a place for everything, as nearly as possible, we ought to find where it is and we ought so to arrange our material. The temptation to the novice is to put his most pertinent material first without consideration of the importance of preparing his audience to receive it.

4. *Next to readiness of your audience to receive what you have to give them, the object you have in view will most frequently determine the order* in which you should present what you have to say. In preaching, a man seeks first to present the truth he believes God has given to him. In the second place, he will remember that preaching this truth has a particular object in view, which is to lead men to embrace that truth and incorporate it in their personalities and conduct. In other words, the preacher seeks to persuade men to become Christ-like. The audience may be in various positions relative to this great object. Some of them have made the initial decision and taken some forward steps toward Christ-likeness. Others in his audience have not considered the first step. Some others may have been so deaf to the word spoken they are utterly ignorant of all that Christianity teaches. Some persons may be listening who are in a state of open rebellion toward God. However different the minds of your auditors may be, sometime in your preaching you will desire to meet the particular state of mind of each and win him to a definite commitment of himself. Facing the diversified elements of time, and condition, and development, which each congregation presents, those which focus on the preacher at the preaching hour he recognizes and endeavors to meet. His methods of approach and content of thought must be fitted to attain his immediate goal. Preaching cannot be effective without this. There are thoughts, illustrations, and types of argument fitted to meet a desired end. They must, therefore, be put in the right order if the desired objective is to be reached.

The observance of order in the arrangement of the content of the sermon avoids confusion—the joining of contradictions and putting the less and the greater in the wrong place. Orderliness is the first law of efficiency. This is as true of a sermon as it is of an army. It should be efficient in the attainment of its goal. Order tends to make the sermon intelligible. Through orderliness the cumulative power of address is increased, whether we consider argument, description, narration, or meditation.

The third quality of an efficient sermon is *movement*. In the vernacular of the day, it is that quality in the sermon that "gets across" what you have to say. The personality of the preacher and his method of delivery have much to do in achieving this.

The quality of thought and the arrangement of the material are also important. Movement describes the spirit and power of advancing thought and feeling in the material, as well as in the preacher, that gives the audience the consciousness of getting toward the goal toward which their vision has been directed. The audience gets the conviction of arriving at a certain destination. They will say of a sermon that has movement, "That gets somewhere." You may remember the amusing description Mark Twain gave of a listener who was moved in the first ten minutes of the preacher's utterance and decided he would give ten dollars to the cause being presented. But the preacher continued speaking, and without progress or movement in his thought. With the extension of his utterance, interest and feeling declined. When the preacher finished instead of putting ten dollars in the plate the listener took out ten cents! Many listeners have had an experience something akin to that. Up to a certain point in the sermon they have felt the preacher was getting somewhere. But when this sense of movement ceased, a revulsion of feeling occurred. Things were going backward and not forward. Every word spoken that does not carry the listener forward may better be left unsaid.

Some suggestions that are helpful in securing movement in the sermon may be made.

1. *Begin with reserve and moderation.* One of the great elements of success in public speaking is the impression of the poise and power of the speaker under the discipline and restraint of his task. He does not allow his feeling to be unleashed with his first utterance. He remembers no one in his audience feels as he feels when he is beginning. He wants to bring them to that. They will never act as he wants them to act until they are aroused. The arousing is what he is to accomplish by an intelligent, passionate, but disciplined utterance of the truth. So the old advice is good: begin low, rise higher, take fire, burn up.

2. *Study the power of condensation.* Prolix, involved statements are seldom blessed with energy and movement. It is the man who has put much in a few words that marches on. A study of commercial letter writing would help some public speakers to gain in brevity and directness. It would teach them to say what it is needful to say in the fewest words. Every speaker who is given to easy speech should write carefully and then use his blue pencil freely.

3. *In descriptions of scenes and events, give the distinctive features.* I have found much help in the study

of cartoons of people. The cartoonist catches the high points and puts them in exaggeration. The features of a man's face may thus become laughable but there is no mistaking the fact that the cartoonist sees the essential characteristics of that face. Sometimes great social and political concepts as well as religious ideas dealt with have thus been made plain and undeniable. I remember two great political leaders, both of whom were known the world over. The first of these was known because of his championship of certain social and political programs. This man went on a world tour and was away from the country for a whole year. When he returned, the cartoonist presented him arriving at the home port confronted by his chief political opponent, who was dressed in the clothes he had left behind but which had been appropriated by the opposition while he was gone. It would have taken political orators hours to prove what the cartoonist set forth with a few exaggerating strokes of his pencil, namely, the complete shift that had been made in the opponent's propaganda.

Let the preacher apply the principles of observation, selection, and discrimination in the use of events and occasions as material for his sermons. In such a process he will eliminate the secondary and unimportant. He will pass rapidly from incident to incident, from one distinctive feature to another.

In argument, the main points of reasons should be so presented the hearer has a mental picture of what is being presented.

Here again the short sentence and unexpanded single-subject-paragraphs, we have previously noticed, contributed to the movement desired.

4. *Develop the points of your sermon proportionate to their importance.* Some will require more consideration than others. Do not judge that each requires the same time or the same length. Sometimes they may; but not often.

5. *It needs to be emphasized that the introductory thoughts be as briefly dealt with as possible.*

When these three qualities of a sermon—*Unity, Order and Movement*—have been sought and found, both hearer and preacher will have reciprocal emotional reactions that indicate the success of the sermon.

CHAPTER IX

STYLE

THERE are three qualities of effective preaching that are treated under the subject of style. In such treatment there is usually more deference for the written word. What we have to say is determined by our interest in effective speaking. The sermon is prepared for a listening audience, not a reading one. Literary values are secondary. If the preacher becomes interested in literary production, the sermon qualities are liable to suffer. Sermons are to be spoken. The main consideration is to utter something for the hour that will move the hearer to a definite course of action—now. If the preacher becomes interested in producing literature, he may, probably will, sacrifice the demands of the hour for the attainment of something that is in the future. "Above all other men," said Henry Ward Beecher, "the preacher should avoid what may be called literary style as distinguished from a natural one and by a 'literary style,' I understand one which abounds in these two elements—the artificial structure of sentences, and the use of words and phrases peculiar to literature alone, and not to common life."[1]

Ozora Davis quotes Brunetiere, "Style is one's manner of expressing himself," and we would add—in public speech. There are three qualities describing ex-

117

cellence in such expression that are called qualities of style, according to Dr. Davis. He names them "Purity," "Precision," and "Clearness." In reference to style, he speaks of it as comparable with the clothes a man wears. The words he chooses are his speech-clothes, which he uses according to sound principles of grammar and in the language of good usage. "Precision" is that quality of exactness that conveys what the author means to convey. "Clearness" is that quality of writing or speech that is immediately plain to all who read or hear.

These are excellent statements; but they seem to describe factors that may be acquired and put on for the occasion without being essentially part and parcel of the man himself. The danger that befalls a man who thinks and strives for style as an objective is artificiality in writing and speaking. Artificiality is hard to be rid of. The opposite of artificiality is naturalness. Naturalness is the thing to be sought in writing and speaking. This can be secured only in the harmonious functioning of the whole man in composition and utterance. "Style," says John Oman, "is not your clothes, but your skin, depending on the health of the whole body, and the proper functioning of which the health of the body depends. The very first quality of style is that it is your own, a true expression of yourself, the fitting vehicle of your particular way of thinking and feeling. Hence taking thought for form effects not a style but a mannerism or even an affectation; and as Schopenhauer says, a style which is not your own is not a face but a mask which in its monotony is more repulsive than the ugliest face."[2]

In common conversation upon this subject I find

when people talk about style in preaching they think not only of the matter of the sermon, the thought of the preacher and the language in which he expresses it, but they think of his manner of expression through voice and gesture—the quality of the voice used, the inflection, the pronunciation, enunciation, emphasis, movement of the hands and body, habits of conduct behind the pulpit desk, his posture before his audience. And doubtless all these have much to do in the preacher's case. But it would be a too inclusive use of the word to undertake a discussion of all these elements when speaking of style in sermon construction and delivery. We shall, therefore, speak of it only in three particulars.

The first of these three qualities of preaching is *clarity*. The word means brightness, brilliance, clearness, that which can be seen through. It means freedom from blurring, without cloudiness or the muddiness that destroys the full form of an object or that brings dimness to the vision.

To secure this quality in the expression of thought, the correct and precise word must be found to express the exact intention or aim of the speaker. "There are no symbols," says Arthur John Gossip, "anything like so wonderful as words, these old things we keep throwing at each other. And beautiful words, and finished English win the heart."[3] The success a man has in securing clarity in his statements will depend upon the purity and choice of his vocabulary. Such words are obtained only at great cost, in the constant reading of literature that embodies them. In a man's early years he should read only those authors whose words are clear. There are such among men who make no claim to a creation of great literature. I am thinking, for example, of such a writer as William Hale White, the author of *Mark Rutherford, His Autobiography and Redemption, Clara Hopgood, Revolution in Tanners Lane,* and other books. You will find on every page of any or all of these the shortest, simplest, purest Anglo-Saxon words. Then there is Charles Lamb, whose writing is familiar to all lovers of English literature for the purity of his style, expressed in the best and simplest speech. Many have given books to the world any one of which would richly reward the man who makes them his serious study. Within the reach of every man are Shakespeare, the Bible, and Bunyan, to which a man determined to secure clarity in speech may turn and read and emulate. Simple, clear, pure, short words, through which his audience can see without a blur and know what the speaker intends to say, should be the preacher's quest. When these become his possession, the very substance of *all* his utterance of thought and life, he gains a style that is clear.

Those who wish to continue the study are referred to DeQuincy and Herbert Spencer's *Essays on Style* and the writings of Phelps, Prof. T. W. Hunt, Prof. John Earle, of Oxford, and those chapters in *Preparation and Delivery of Sermons* on the subject of style by Dr. Broadus. Also *On Reading Books,* by John Livingston Lowes.

Words are the vehicles of thought, and a man must think clearly. When he does, then he must choose his words that are connected with the history of thought expression at its best. Nothing can take the place of clarity of thought. But there are many words a man may use to express himself—words that have different origins and associations. English words have behind them a history of long association with the English mind. These are the words for Englishmen and Americans to find and treasure and use.

The second quality of good speaking style is *beauty*. If we may use the figure of clothes, it satisfies the sense of correctness—harmony in color, in form and proportion. In the sermon, beauty is that quality that appeals to the loftiest and best, the true and the good in men. It is adherence to the standard Christ embodies. A beautiful style is true to the Master and the Revelation He brought. It is attained when the Preacher and his message are true to what He was, to what He said, and what He did.

There is a Biblical phrase that is currently used expressing the opposite of the thing we are trying to describe, i.e., "conformity to the world." Conformity to the world is unbecoming to the minister. The sermon of a man conformed to the world will lack "the mind of Christ." A sermon should express the mind of Christ, to secure the beauty we are talking about. If it does not do this, it lacks one important quality.

It may at first seem to be a decided descent in this discussion to say that to secure beauty in style a man's words must make a good impression on the ear, but Henry Ward Beecher insisted that words and phrases must be chosen that sound well on the ear and gain the attention thereby. This is only to conform to beauty in the standard of sound. Harsh speaking, either in spirit or in words, is not beautiful. There are doubtless occasions when beauty may well be sacrificed for the sake of awakening and rebuking the careless and indifferent. Such occasions are usually indicated. But they are exceptions that prove the rule. The type of utterance a man should seek and strive to attain is speech that is pleasing to the ear.

I want to give one illustration of beauty in style. It is taken from Arthur John Gossip's great sermon on "The Galilean Accent." "Once on a day in France the bonniest of experiences befell me. I suppose in the Middle Ages they would certainly have said that I saw Jesus Christ with my very own eyes. And perhaps I did. We had been weeks in that appalling desolation up toward Paschendaele where there was never a blade of grass, nor any tree, only that empty, woesome land churned into miles and miles of shellholes, till it looked like some wild tumbling sea. And at long last we had gone back to rest. And it seemed heaven. For there were budding hedgerows, and a glimmer of green on living trees, and grass and flowers, glorious flowers in the first splendor of the spring. And one's dry soul lay greedily soaking in the sheer beauty of it all. And the next day news came that we were needed back in the old place of horror, to be thrown into a losing battle. It reached us on a perfect afternoon of sunshine; and, with heart grown hot and hard, I had turned down a lovely little lane with a brown burn wimpling beside it, and a lush meadow, all brave sheets of golden and purple flowers on either side. The earth was very beautiful; and life seemed very sweet; and it was hard to go back into the old purgatory and face death again. And with that, through a gap in a hedge there came a shepherd laddie tending his flock of some two dozen sheep. He was not driving them in our rough way with barking dogs. But he went first and they were following him; and if one loitered, he called it by name and it came running to him. So they moved on down the lane, and up a little hill, up the brow, and over it, and so out of my life. And I stood staring after them, hearing as if the words were spoken out aloud to me and to me only, 'And when He putteth forth His sheep, He goeth before them,' turned and went down the land to face what was to be with a heart quieted and stilled. 'Has not God brought me here?' said Christ: 'has not He brought me to this hour?' And He is a good shepherd, wise and kind, and very tender, who makes no mistakes."[4]

The third of these excellent qualities that make for a good style and for effective preaching is *force*, which includes precision and energy. It is that which we link or identify with a man's "capacity for exercising influence or producing an effect." It describes the effectiveness with which the man himself is carried over and communicated to those to whom he speaks. It is the dynamic quality of personality-weight of manhood, measure of vital energy that is an inherent quality of the man that flows out in his speech. It is that ruggedness of life that lends energy to a man's utterance because it is an essential part of his nature. Force is the vital power for accomplishing work—especially the work of convincing others, and that lends strength and impulse to the power of persuasion. It increases valiancy in the face of opposition, courage in adventurous living for Christ and humanity. It is the impact power in preaching that describes a man of weight.

Such men as possess force give inspiration to the oppressed and aid them in rising up against oppression. They have valiancy for those whose cause has been overwhelmed or lost. They give new hope to those who despair of victory.

Men without force can do little for such needy ones. They do not have the quality in themselves that gives strength and stability in the face of temptation and can *not* give it to others.

Forceful men have the trumpet note in their speech. Force describes their carriage in the walk of life. Their sermons express this quality of force because it describes the man. He lives forcefully.

Insofar as the truth of the gospel is involved in the work of preaching, the measure in which that truth has been accepted by the preacher will lend additional power in his preaching. He gains in authority by it and increase of power and influence. Men will be convinced of sin because the preacher is convinced of sin. Men will be convinced of truth because the preacher is convinced of truth. Men will be inspired to live grandly because the preacher lives grandly. Men will venture in faith because the preacher dares to venture in faith.

These are qualities of personality, woven into the warp and woof of the sermon by the preacher who possesses them. They are something that cannot be put into utterance unless they are in the preacher. They cannot be put into the sermon by one who adheres to creeds, and liturgies, and rules, however glibly they may be recited, unless they have become the substance of his personality.

Take the notable example, Moody. What made him
so great in his effect upon men? It was the weight of
his impact as a man. He was a man of force. He
may have violated many of the rules of homiletics,
but those he observed gained in the weight of his personality. Moody was greater than all the rules. In
him they gained in force, coming to their best expression in what he said.

Force was the dominant quality of Henry Ward
Beecher, and it was increased in the profuse employment of his illustrations. He gathered his illustrations
from the broad fields of human life and interest, from
science, business, philosophy, literature, from poverty
and toil, from wealth and comfort, from sorrow and
joy, from pain and happiness, from all life; and the
common people heard him gladly.

I take another illustration from Arthur John Gossip's
sermon, "On the Edge of the Crowd": "Once far up
the duckboard tracks to Paschendaele, in that wild
land churned into a wilderness of shell-holes, like a
tumbling, never resting sea, I came on a dead laddie,
lying all alone. Why, out of all the multitudes one
saw he so affected me, I do not know. But he was
Scottish, and he was young and very handsome and
somebody's dearest. And, somehow, the dead eyes
seemed to look up into mine with solemn challenge;
and the dead lips to cry aloud till my heart heard,
'This is my body broken for you.' And there we
had a communion service of a kind, just we three,
the Lord Jesus, the dead laddie, and my soul; and
I swore that because he had died for us, please God,
I would be worthier that sacrifice. And face to face
with Jesus on the cross, can you turn away?"[5]

Who could escape the power of such preaching? Who could hear or read such utterance and inquiry and not be moved? In those words there is something more than a mere combination of words that describe clarity of statement and beauty of expressions or description. There is carried over to us the power, the force of the personality who conceived them and into whose soul the iron of experience had entered.

In answer to the question—How may an effective style be attained? I think it is clear that my first answer is—develop the man that is in you. The sermon's quality and power will never be better than the man's. Men who have been rascals have written books that are described by clarity, beauty, and force as literature. They have spoken on occasions with the same grandeur. Nevertheless, we insist that sermons cannot gain that impact that persuades men to become Christlike, with that effectiveness that leads men to accept Jesus Christ and incorporate Him into their lives, unless the preacher has accepted and incorporated Him in his life. He who would develop the good style must find and incorporate the good, the true, and the beautiful in himself. Style is the man. So the first rule for the development of style in preaching is to develop oneself in these excellencies.

Other rules have been stated, that if observed, will facilitate a man's progress in such a process. Arthur John Gossip gives us laws from Schopenhauer:

1. "Have something to say," which, he observes, "was Sir Walter Scott's opinion almost in the same words. 'Get ideas and words will come.'"

2. "Write carefully. A man who writes carelessly at once confesses that he puts no great value on his thoughts."

3. " 'Seek clear, comprehensive and unambiguous words'—a Socratic injunction."

4. "State the naked, simple truth."[6]

Beecher, who thought of his audience and the purpose of a sermon as an instrument to move them to action, according to Crocker[7] had four elements to consider as determining style:

1. Words and idioms of every-day speech.
2. The sentence rhythmical and direct.
3. Qualities—plain language that pleases the people; bell-notes which ring out.
4. Concepts, suggestions to the popular mind, definite and picturesque that awaken them to think and act.

All teachers of style emphasize what we have before emphasized, the importance of acquiring a vocabulary of short, pithy words—words that are in common use. To take up Gossip again: "There are no symbols anything like so wonderful as words, these odd things we keep throwing at each other." "And beautiful words and finished English win the heart. Style is not idle. It is power. Time spent upon it is not wasted; the mere suggestion is crime. For a phrase, an image, an apt adjective, may bring home to some needy soul a whole new side of truth, may make it feel God very near, may win it for the Master. It is often through such things that these great matters happen. It is the added master-touch that makes it vivid, runs it into the mind, the heart, the conscience."[8]

We conclude therefore, that the man who seeks to preach efficient sermons must give earnest attention to these qualities of style we designate as *clarity*, *beauty*, and *force*.

Chapter X

SPECIES, OR TYPES, OF SERMONS

Teachers of homiletics differ in their classification of sermons. It makes little difference which teacher is followed. The principal thing to remember is— seek variety in the subject matter and in the method of presenting the truth. Guard against monotony. Evangelical preachers must present the love of God revealed in Christ to the world. But even the continuous presentation of the love of God may become commonplace and uninteresting if the same method is continuously followed.

Likewise also, the second coming of our Lord is a great Biblical theme; but it is not the whole of New Testament truth and should not be the only message of any preacher. Men who are tempted to the overemphasis of any one great theme should remember the Gospels and Epistles are compendiums of many great themes all of which should have their place and time for proclamation. And in the presentation of these evangelical themes no preacher should neglect or pass by the great moral and ethical subjects continuously recurring in the Bible as he speaks in an age that has lost its way.

There are problems that have to be faced in a socially and politically corrupt time. No social redemption can be achieved and no government established, unless the prophets of God cry aloud until their warfare against wickedness in high places be accomplished. Thus a variety of subjects call for a preacher's utterance. He cannot accomplish his work without a consideration of these great themes and a proclamation of them in a variety of ways.

In his *Preparation and Delivery of Sermons*, Broadus classifies subjects as "Doctrinal," "Moral," "Historical," "Experimental"; "sermons for special occasions and classes: funeral, academic, anniversary, revival, to children and other special classes." He speaks of sermons as "Subject Sermons," "Text Sermons," and "Expository Sermons."[1] In his *The Ideal Ministry*, Johnson has three groups—"explanatory, observational, and propositional."[2] Others present different classifications. From all these, according to their individual or personal method and outlook, the multiplied types are indicated.

The type of sermon a man should use will be determined by the occasion, or by the answer he makes to the question: How can I best approach this audience so as to accomplish my purpose now?

I am thinking now of the death of a theological professor and the funeral message spoken at the seminary chapel. The preacher took the opportunity to set forth, as clearly as he could, the essential gospel to which the departed had given years of his life, in preparing young men to preach. No message that preacher ever had spoken was more appropriately uttered than what he spoke on that funeral occasion when the body of a faithful preacher and teacher of that gospel lay in his casket before the pulpit. Only once or twice did he mention the name of the Professor. He talked only about that to which the professor had devoted his life.

That sermon was definitely a doctrinal sermon, an apologetic presentation of the essential gospel message to the audience and the world to which he spoke. Nothing else could have been more fit. Men and women went away conscious of the grandeur of a life devoted to the promulgation of such a message to the world.

Now it is evident doctrinal sermons may be of different kinds: narrative, descriptive, propositional, biographical, or other types. It is only required that the doctrine presented be so clearly indicated or outlined in the subject matter it will be easily discerned by those to whom the message is brought. The kind of an audience to which a man speaks will have something to do with the language he uses and the type of sermon he selects for the presentation of the message.

Object sermons, as some are called, are those in which some object or picture or device is used as the illustration of the principle thought the preacher wishes to press home to his listener's minds. I remember a sermon preached to the Sunday school, which attended a Sunday service in a body. It was on "The Traps that Catch Men." After some hesitation, the preacher decided in his preparation hours to use a huge bear-trap for his object or illustration. When preaching he talked about the text first and the experience the Scripture describes. He told of different kinds of traps hunters and sportsmen use for various purposes. This led him to refer to this huge heavy-jawed trap fastened against the wall where all could see it. At the right moment, standing at a proper distance, he hurled a piece of 2″ x 4″ scantling at the trigger of the trap and sprang it. The heavy jaws of the trap closed and buried their rough edges into the wood.

The preacher was in doubt about the propriety of this sensational performance until a day or two after, when he heard some boys playing outside, quarreling. One boy lost his temper and spoke violently. The preacher heard the other boys cry out, "The bear trap has got you; the bear trap has got you!" Then he was sure the sermon on "Traps that Catch Men" was successful.

It is not necessary to illustrate farther. Pictures, simple mechanical devices, simple experiments in chemistry, blackboard chalk talks and various objects have, when used as the principal instruments of illustration, made object sermons interesting and effective in the presentation of the truth. Some men preach a five- or ten-minute sermon to children every Sunday, using this type of sermon.

One minister I know preached to the children one Sunday morning each month. The entire service arranged for children occupied one hour. The children occupied the pews in the central block of the audience room. So popular were these "children's" sermons, the problem of finding seats for adult listeners that came in increasing number, became difficult of solution. These were not always object sermons.

This minister used the *Story Form* more frequently than the object sermon. Successful story telling, which involves Bible records, depends upon a familiar acquaintance with the background of events or characters used. The times and customs involved must be understood. The local situation, in which the characters dealt with live and move, must be familiarized. The soil in which the Bible ideals and concepts of successful living are rooted, the atmosphere that surrounds the character involved, have to be studied. Of course it requires a development of the historical and constructive imagination in the preacher, and, withal, a discernment of what is essential in the situation he undertakes to build up. But, if these assets are found in a speaker, the narrative and story form of message production can become most attractive and be made equally unforgettable, and both comforting or bothering to the conscience. I know of a minister once preaching to a very smug, prosperous congregation on "Fruitless Fig-trees" (Luke 13:6-9). His description of the wise and patient gardener, pleading with his master to give him one more season to make the fig-tree productive, was so vivid that a man casually visiting the church was moved by the mercy of God portrayed. He suddenly rose from his pew, walked down the aisle, told the preacher he was the sinner being described and said he wanted to confess his sin and accept Jesus as his Savior then and there. The sudden and unheard of interruption of their service so aroused this congregation that it was the beginning of a revival of religion in the church.

I once heard a *biographical sermon* preached to the faculty and students of an educational institution, that I shall long remember. The preacher was a student of personality and possessed a keen talent for discovering and isolating such personality traits in Old Testament characters. He dealt with three characters closely connected with David as presented in certain

chapters in I Kings. He *also* found the personality
traits of these three men in modern characters. The
comparisons were clear and direct. Of course he
never mentioned by name any particular counterparts
in modern life, but there were people present who must
have gone away wondering how the preacher found
out about them.

The *observational sermon* is another type. The
preacher stands as a witness to what is before him
and tells what he observes. Suppose it is the voyage
of Paul described in Acts 27. His purpose is to tell
about the conduct of Paul on that occasion. He thoroughly acquaints himself with the details of the ship—
its captain and crew, their treatment and attitude
toward their prisoner guest, the people who accompanied them, the hazards they faced in the voyage, the
storm that swept suddenly and furiously down upon
them, the efforts made to face the storm and their disposition of the cargo, the fasting and prayer in which
they engaged, and the darkness and tempest that overwhelmed them. In all these situations Paul was competent to advise and lead them. He put the spirit
of good cheer into them. He made bold declaration
of the divine guidance he received. He declared his
faith and confidence in this guidance. He expressed
courageous allegiance to God and God's purpose for
him and them. Observing such a man, the preacher
will be able to describe a type of leadership that is
needed for every storm-tossed generation.

Observations may be made on any form of statement used as a text, as Dr. Johnson indicates in his
treatment of the text, "Grow in grace of our Lord and
Savior Jesus Christ." In such cases, the preacher

becomes a commentator. His observations are not presented in the form of an argument but as valuable considerations. He leaves the result to the weight and intrinsic value the observation may possess.

The treatment a man may make of any text, as we have learned, will be largely determined by the very nature of the text itself or as the occasion calls for. It would seem if a man faces a situation that is unfriendly the observational type of sermon made in the manner of a commentator offers a way of approach, to be followed later by a definite propositional treatment of the same subject. In the second type, the forensic method — stating a definite proposition and proving it to the satisfaction of the reason, he will lay a solid foundation for strong and passionate appeals for the acceptance and practice of what is reasonable. In this, Dr. Herrick Johnson was a master among preachers. The criticism or comment one feels disposed to offer of the sermon plans he presents in "The Ideal Ministry," on the text (II Pet. 3:18), is that the explanatory and observational are too much like the propositional in both form and method. In the hands of Dr. Johnson they were doubtless not so, but in the hands of less capable men they would appear too much as a distinction without a difference.

The observational sermon is particularly adapted to historical events recorded in the Scripture, in which great personages appear and act courageously and valiantly, where great deeds are wrought in courage, faith, hope, and cheer; where a man acts as though he believes in God and loves his fellow-man. The preacher describes convictions that are basic in the building of great personality. He discovers and il-

luminates these in references to conduct that is desirable in any person but especially in leaders of men.

In the early years of a man's preaching the *propositional sermon* is a desirable type of sermon to use
most frequently.   Such preaching develops exactness
in the statement of the theme—the subject he proposes to present.   It leads to a careful analysis of
the subject.   It calls upon him to state definitely each
division of his sermon.   He gains in the strengthening
of his logical faculty.   It calls for an orderly presentation of the argument he makes and enables him to
appreciate the cumulative value of strong and effective speech.

In the proposition he clearly states the subject and
the task he proposes to accomplish.   To return to the
illustration of this type of sermon Dr. Johnson offered.
The same text referred to before is the one considered
(II Pet. 3:18).   His theme is "Growth in Grace is
a Christian Duty," and the outline is as follows:

"I.   Because commanded of God.
"II.   Because growth is a law of all healthful life.
"III.   Because increase of grace is increase of power.
        Speech is might as it has character behind it.
"IV.   Because the more we grow Christ-like, the
        more we honor Christ."

The propositional sermon is a type of sermon that
is calculated to set forth strong successive reasons,
that become for personality like beams in the structure
of a building by which the strength and stability of
the whole structure are established.   It makes the development of the proposition easy to remember, and
a man carries it with him in the after days and months
and even years.

A word must be added in favor of so-called *doctrinal preaching*, which, in these later years has been neglected. We use the word doctrine in its primary meaning as a teaching, a truth that is held. It is not necessarily a dogma, though it may be. A doctrine may be part of a creed. The creed is a formal statement of a truth or a number of truths in systematic relation to each other, and which, all together, make up an organized whole. The creed, founded upon Scriptural teachings, presents a number of truths, which are repeatedly expressed or implied throughout the various parts of that Scripture. The preacher presenting a doctrinal sermon devotes his message to the exposition of some particular truth he finds embodied in one of the great passages of the Word of God. Necessarily, it is a clear and positive statement of that truth that he begins with. The sermon is an unfolding of that truth. When he believes its acceptance as stated is necessary to salvation, without the acceptance of which he would deny membership in a given group of believers called a church, it becomes a dogma and the preacher dogmatic in its presentation.

But such dogmatism is not necessary to doctrinal preaching. It is doctrinal preaching when a particular truth is clearly and definitely presented. Such preaching is fundamental to the development of Christian character; for, without definite declaration of truth that clearly sets Christ before people, such character is not possible. The correctness and comprehensiveness of presenting Christ will determine the magnitude, strength, and beauty to which Christian character may be developed.

The failure of men to preach doctrinal sermons will

always be followed by an inability in the people to
state what they mean by the words Christian, forgiveness, salvation, repentance, conversion, sanctification,
or even what Christianity, in a Biblical sense, really
is. One of the notable passages in literature illustrating the misfortune that describes those who have not
been doctrinally instructed is found in that auto-
biographical work of John Ruskin known as *The
Praterita,* and the full text of which was set out in
a previous chapter. Ruskin, you will recall, was observing the crowd passing before the pictures in a
great gallery of Christian art. They were utterly unable to appreciate and understand this art, because
they did not know what Christianity is. He followed
his observation of their ignorance and inability to appreciate the glorious pictures with a definition of
Christianity. In that definition he stated some of the
greatest truths contained in the Scriptures touching
the person of Christ these people must know in order
to appreciate Christian art.

One can easily discover the misfortune that has befallen the present generation by asking any professed
Christian to define Christianity or to say what he
means by "sin," or "salvation," or "prayer," "repentance," "forgiveness," or a number of words that
are in the common vocabulary of professed followers
of Christ.

It is the duty of preachers to instruct the people
in these great fundamental teachings of the Christian
faith. Without such instructional, doctrinal preaching,
Christianity becomes anemic and flabby and wanting
in conviction and power.

If a man takes up the study of the Scriptures and

steadily advances in a knowledge of the truth of God, of Christ, and of the Holy Spirit, God's attitude toward man and man's attitude toward God, himself and his fellow-men, he will be able, not only to win them, but to build them up in this "faith once delivered to the saints"—enable them to live valiantly in the expression of that faith and ultimately advance the kingdom of God in the world.

It may be well to give one more example of such preaching. The text is, "Who gave Himself for our sins" (Gal. 1:4—the first clause of the verse). The purpose of the sermon is to convince the hearer of the curse of sin and the saving power of Jesus Christ. The preacher began by observing the difficulties that confront us today in our ignorance or denial of the fact of sin.

I. *He noted the tendency of current thought about sin.*

(1) The tendency to belittle and decry the teaching of the fact.

(2) The public tolerance of sin in individuals.

(3) The current teaching that it is nothing but social maladjustment, or mental ill health.

II. *The Bible teaching on the subject.*

(1) Sin is the darkest and most destructive thing to personality in human experience.

(2) Escape from it requires a Redeemer, who can reach down and in loving, sacrificial purpose deliver from its power.

Jesus Christ is such a person.

(1) He was without sin.

(2) He loved the sinner.

(3) He set Himself in direct opposition to sin and
    gave His life for the redemption of the sinner.

Our inability to understand the mystery does not destroy the fact any more than our ignorance of radio
activity and construction limits our capacity to use it.

III. *We know it is a fact that Jesus Christ saves
from sin.*

(1) Because Jesus declares this is what He came
    to do.
(2) His disciples testify to the fact that He saves
    from sin.
(3) Witnesses can be found in every age and many
    lands to witness to the fact.

Again, there is the *occasional sermon*. Let us take
one occasion to which every minister is asked, at some
time, to appear and preach, i.e., on the ordination of
a young man to the gospel ministry. The demand of
such an occasion may be met with a variety of subjects.
For example, the preacher on one occasion dealt with
the situation all preachers confront in their day, with
the unusual text: Matt. 26: 62-63: "And the high priest
arose, and said unto him, I adjure thee by the living
God, that thou tell us whether thou be the Christ, the
Son of God." His theme was "Our World Confronts
our Religion." His purpose was to indicate responsibility that rests on the preacher.

Introduction—There are two distinct lessons in this
record:

(a) There are some issues we do not need to answer.
(b) There are questions that must be faced and an-
    swered. Not to answer is to deny the truth,
    belittle the gospel, and prove disloyal to the
    gospel.

Our world confronts us with four such questions and the preacher must make answer. It asks:

I. Do you have a Revelation from God? And the preacher must make answer that we do.

II. Is God available for the tragic needs of human frailty? And we must answer yes, to that.

III. Is death the disaster to personality it seems to be? And we must answer it is not.

IV. Does religion have ethical significance to society, economics, or politics? And we must show that it does.

Conclusion: Men must face the Christian faith, then, as a practical, imperative issue and accept the answer it makes and incorporate its teaching in their personalities and lives.

Such is the preacher's vocation. He is an ambassador for Jesus Christ to a world that needs Him and His message.

The installation of a minister is an occasion when a biographical type of sermon may be used. Take such a text as John 1: 6-7: "There was a man sent from God whose name was John." On this occasion the preacher dealt with five qualities in the personality of John the Baptist, who was "A God-Sent Man":

1. A man of courage. He faced the Pharisees and Sadducees bravely (Matt. 3:7-8)

2. A preacher of repentance (Matt. 3: 7-12)

3. A man of humility (Matt. 3: 13-14; John 1: 27)

4. A man of religious interest and perception (Matt. 11:9)

5. A man whom God chose for a great task (John 1:6-7—to bear witness to the Light). Such a man must be sincere, guileless, transparent.

It is not necessary that a man use so many headings but it is important, as the preacher understood, that a man of genuine, manly, virile strength should be found to serve as a preacher.

We follow a good example in giving a third illustration of a sermon outline for this occasion of inducting a minister into office as pastor and preacher to a community; the subject: "What the Minister stands for in the community," and the text Acts 10: 42: "And he commanded us to preach unto the people, and to testify that this is He which was ordained of God to be the Judge of the quick and dead."

Introduction: This portion of Scripture presents the Apostle's warrant for preaching. It is the command of Christ Himself. And just in proportion to the completeness with which a preacher strips away all other considerations till he comes to the conviction, and sees Christ clearly, and hears Him speak directly, and indicates his preaching function specifically, will he preach authoritatively (see I Cor. 1:17).

I. *The preacher stands in the community, then, as the representative of Jesus Christ.* His power will depend upon the measure with which he accepts this limitation.

II. *The preacher stands for the revelation of God in the terms of human personality.*

Therefore, the experience of the fact of God is an experience possible to human personality. This experience becomes the primary qualification of the preacher. He witnesses to this great fact.

III. *The preacher witnesses to the obligation that we must get the spirit of Christ into our human relationships.*

The lordship of Jesus Christ depends not only on

the relation He sustained to the Father, but upon the completeness with which He carried His own spirit into every relation of life.

(a) He never taught a duty He did not live up to.

(b) He never met an opposition He did not master.

(c) He never failed a soul who trusted in Him.

Conclusion: Our duty cannot be accomplished in the world until we get His will incorporated into the institutions and relationship which life encompasses. And for this the preacher must stand in every community to which he ministers.

There are also such occasions as the *graduating exercises* of schools, colleges, and universities. Each occasion presents its peculiar and distinct challenge. It seems to me the man who speaks to men and women who are facing the end of their educational history in college and graduate-institutions, deals with those to whom some of the great essential truths of the Christian faith may be clearly and pleadingly presented. I have found it has been most highly commended by both faculty and students when such a course has been followed. Too many preachers to such audiences attempt to deal with subjects that lie within the purview of academic chairs, for which they are not fitted, and thus miss the opportunity of preaching what the occasion presents. In the secondary schools the biographical type of sermon is very acceptable. The challenge to earnest and noble living is the type of subjects most effective. I give one illustration of a sermon preached to a high-school audience. The subject was suggested by the large letters seen on the sweaters of students it is the custom of colleges to award to those who have proved themselves worthy to receive such honors. The message

was learned from reading many times the letters of an
old man to his spiritual son in the faith.—I Tim. 1: 2:
"Unto Timothy, my own son in the faith." The theme:
"A four letter man." Introduction dealt with the com-
radeship of these two men. The message was on what
the younger received from the older man:

I. Courage—"Be of good courage."

II. Culture—"Study to show thyself approved."

III. Concentration—"This one thing I do."

IV. Conscience—"Holding faith and a good conscience, which some having thrust from them
made shipwreck."

In illustration of what may be presented to a university audience, the particular sermon referred to was
on "The Preeminence of Christ," and was a presentation of the personality of our Lord and what He was
to God and the world.

Political sermons are occasionally called for—that
is, sermons that have to do with the great interests of
public welfare or good citizenship and which may be
presented on notable historic anniversaries. One might
discuss the subject of loyalties, or allegiance to government, or the perplexity of righteous leadership. Here
are plans for such subjects on texts taken from the
Book of Joshua:

Josh. 1: 16-18. Loyalty to administration is shown in:

I. Obedience to lawfully selected leaders.

II. Prayer for their divine guidance.

III. Insistence upon the enforcement of authority.

IV. Speaking encouragingly to it and for it.

Then again, on *the perplexity of righteous leadership*—the way to follow—Josh. 7: 8: "O Lord, what

shall I say, when Israel turneth their backs before their enemies!"

    I. Take an erect attitude toward the situation.

    II. Purify the body politic.

    III. Obey the will of God.

On "The Question of Allegiance" (Josh. 5:13):

    I. It was answered by considering their relation to God: "as captain of the host of the Lord am I now come."

    II. It was answered with an appreciation of the environment.

    III. It was answered with a symbol of valiancy and war upon the enemies of the Lord.

One must face the fact that the pertinency of all such preaching is definitely affected by the particular environment, time, occasion, and character of the personages and elements involved, so that such sermon plans can be little more than an indication of lines to be followed. One can only make suggestions and offer examples for general observation.

CHAPTER XI

THE MINISTER'S STUDY

THERE are certain considerations that must be kept
in the mind of the preacher and the public to whom
he ministers. The preacher of the gospel is the one
man in the community who is looked to as "the authority," the recognized expert in religion. Such position cannot be maintained unless he is religious and
intelligent. Intelligence cannot be maintained without
reading, meditation, and some creative thinking. Religion cannot be cultivated without daily contact with
God, study of, and meditation upon His Word. Therefore, the minister must have a study in which he spends
the best hours of every day.

I. *As to its location.* It ought to be accessible to
anyone who wants to reach him when he needs him.
But, on the other hand, it ought to be apart from the
interruptions to which life is constantly subjected. It
should be large enough to house the necessary books
and the necessary instruments for solid work. It may
be in the church or his home, preferably in his home.
Since so much of his time must be spent in it, good
light and ventilation, warmth in winter and coolness in
summer, are important.

It ought also to guarantee to him quiet and privacy.
"No real thinking can be done in the vicinity of noise,"

146

said Herbert Spencer. Men who have developed the
power of concentration of the mind in the midst of
noise know this dictum is sound, not to mention the
experience of men who have *had* to think as best they
could in the vicinity of noise.

II. Every preacher's study should be equipped with
a desk or table at which he can face his work. A comfortable chair is important, as the time spent at his
desk is not the best time to suffer hardship. Good pen-
cils and a ready pen, with a supply of scratch-paper
pads, should be always within reach, as well as paper
for manuscript work.

A good common-place book should be at hand in
which to write his own reflections on themes for future
use and in which he may record the valuable contributions others make, which he discovers in his reading.

A well-bound copy of the Bible, with wide margins
or interleaved clean white pages, for his study work,
is most desirable. He may use this same copy for his
private and devotional readings. On the margin, or
interleaved pages, he may record his own reflections
on the passages read and make references to his collateral study in commentaries and other books. In time
he will have special volumes for his pulpit, or public
use, and other special purposes, but in the earlier years
the constant use of a single volume is not a drawback
to him.

Close at hand should be good commentaries, never
homiletic ones at the beginning. They become dangerous to his own creative-power development. Commentaries that help him to understand the meaning of
words and grammatical constructions are the ones to
secure. Let him begin with those on the Gospels, some

good commentary on the Psalms and on the Major Prophets; later, a study of the Acts and the Epistles, adding such commentaries as teachers can or have suggested. We would advise against the purchase of sets in early years of purchasing. All volumes in such sets are seldom the "best" on all the books they treat. Books on the parables may be added later. Buy commentaries slowly and carefully.

We would strongly advise that the young preacher master his Bible one book at a time. We remember the story of the old Scotchman who observed he "had found the Bible a mighty good book on the commentaries." Nevertheless, commentaries that help a man to know who wrote the Bible text, for whom it was written, and what is really said in the writing, will seldom be greatly disappointed even when he interrogates his commentary on some text he wants to use next Sunday and does not find much said on that particular text.

Next to these important tools, the study should have a good and "unabridged" dictionary, with a thesaurus easy to handle, and a book on synonyms and antonyms, for the preacher must be a student of words, of their origin and root meanings, and so far as possible, their use. He must seek to know also their correct pronunciation. No virtue in public speaking takes precedence over the use of proper words, their correct and accepted pronunciation and clear enunciation.

In selecting books that engage his study hours, let him remember some master in the use of short, sharp, Anglo-Saxon words should find a place among the first in his list. His authorized King James Version of the Bible, a good readable volume of Shakespeare, and

Bunyan's *Pilgrim's Progress*, should certainly be among his early purchases and his constant companions. Every preacher should have some field of thought with which he is particularly conversant and in which he comes to be something of a specialist. There are great fields of study in which he must constantly read, such as Old and New Testament literature, history, philosophy, apologetics, missions; some fields in which he is particularly interested, be it poetry, biography, essays, fiction; and these books he will buy. Only four days ago, I listened to one of the recognized masters of pulpit utterance. He had returned to his alma mater to deliver the principal address at the induction of a new president to office in that college. His address upon that occasion was characterized not only by sound thinking upon his subject but by adornment in references and quotations over a wide range of intellectual reading interest and beautified by quotable passages from the choicest poetry. His ability to make such an address was based upon his arduous toil since the day of his graduation some forty years previously. His library is described by quality and not by the number of books on the shelves. *He* is described by an intimate knowledge of what is in those books. It cannot be too often repeated to young men in the ministry—it is not the number of books you possess, but the intimate acquaintance with great books that matters. Make up your mind to know thoroughly each volume you purchase, to purchase the best, and only what you can read. Get those books that are of value after the years have passed.

III. *The minister's study should be dedicated to hard work.* From the beginning of his ministry, the preacher should have a definite early morning hour to enter his study. He should develop the habit of remaining there certain hours of the day at work. Many interruptions will come that cannot be foreseen and that cannot be escaped, but they should not be permitted to divert him from the high purpose to study. Not less than four hours each day and as many more as possible should be devoted to the work in this dedicated task. There is hardly a parish in the land that cannot be trained to respect the time devoted to this purpose. If most men would remain in their study until three, then devote the remainder of the afternoon and evening to the public pastoral visitation, public meetings and committee work for the first ten years of their ministry, they would be able to prepare for and meet the reasonable requirements of any parish. If, then, his work is scheduled and properly distributed in assignment to the definite task of reading, study, and writing, in preparation for his public duties, then a man will be equipped to serve faithfully those who look to him for instruction, inspiration, comfort, and leadership. Certain hours will be set aside for Bible study, certain hours for collateral reading, and certain hours for systematic study of history, theology, philosophy, or some other great field. Men and women have wrought and produced values in these fields for the enrichment of those who are to speak to the people. Living systematically, with certain hours devoted to definite subjects, will enable any man in the course of years to be intelligent and competent to lead, edify, comfort, and inspire his hearers. All men cannot be great in functioning thus. All men are not great. But all men can be useful.

As I write these words my mind recalls the practice of Gamaliel Bradford. Handicapped by ill health, with only a few hours to work in each day, nevertheless he carefully planned and jealously guarded his time. Definite portions of it were given to writing, to reading, to language study, and to music. By this practice he was able to produce scores of articles and books for publication.

Men will differ in the distribution of their time and in the choice of subjects to which they devote their strength. No schedule of subjects and designation of time allotted to each could be profitably worked out for general application, but working out such a schedule for oneself, and rigidly disciplining oneself in adhering to it, is the important duty.

The danger that besets the preacher on the one hand is mental lackadaisicality, and overdevotion to books on the other. The first begets emptiness of mind; the second tends to bookishness, nervous exhaustion, and mental distempers. Either leaves him unfit to preach to men. Because we know that many men excuse their neglect of their study and that many think superficially and ineffectively, it seems necessary to stress the importance of rigid adherence to definite planning and constant devotion to the study. American ministers are not often accused of bookishness. Many of them break down through attempting to be busy on too long a battle-front. They do not husband their time and strength for the main task. Civic and ecclesiastical committees, outside occasions such as luncheon clubs and social engagements, divert them from their desks and they come to their pulpits unprepared. With others, physical

strength, vibrant personality, and charming natural gifts
enable them to meet many speaking engagements without immediate preparation. As the years pass by, they
begin to die at the top. While the reputation they have
established for popular address may carry them on,
nevertheless they are sounding brass and tinkling cym-
bals. Such men have failed in the end.

IV. *The study should be the sanctum sanctorum of
the minister's personal life.* Let him establish the habit
of beginning the day with at least the first half-hour
devoted to Bible reading for refreshment of his own
soul and in the practice of the presence of God for
his own spiritual upbuilding. This is the time and
place to learn Jesus Christ in prayer and worship. As
he reads the Bible, some great truths will flash from
the page and he will talk with God about that. Here
he can discover the shallowness or the emptiness of
his own vessel and have it filled at the fountain. Here
he can bring the needs of his people and find guidance
and direction in dealing with them. Here he will come
in touch with Reality and be equipped to speak with
authority. Here he will learn his Bible, in the presence
and authority of Him who has revealed Himself to
men in past ages. Here he gets insight and understanding. That first hour gives him power to penetrate the
deep things of God and men. Such men pour living
water from fountains of truth when they speak. Such
men will not be dependent upon what the so-called
authorities have uttered. They, themselves, become authorities to whom men will resort, to whom they will
listen. Such a man focuses religion in himself and
makes it the dominant thought for the week in the
lives of his hearers.

Within a week I have been told of such a man and
the sermon he preached. One of the officers of the
church in which he had spoken the previous Sabbath,
but who was not present, said he had heard from his
own family and "many others who were present" of
the great sermon preached that day. The secret of such
a sermon was hid in the vision the preacher caught in
the study where he prepared to proclaim the message.
God revealed it to him in the hours of tryst with Him.

V. *The study should be also the place for his
"clinical" work with seeking souls.* People with whom
the preacher lives and for whom he labors, like to know
the privilege of such a room. There they know they
can put off all pretense and camouflage, unafraid. It
is a place dedicated to the secrets of the Lord, where
they can uncover their lives without fear. Looking back
over the years, one recalls some of the visitors who came
to his study. Once that business man who considered
himself rich. But reverses came. A blanket mortgage
covered everything he possessed. Creditors and business associates hounded and criticized him on every
hand because he remained faithful to his principle of
using a tithe of what he earned for the Lord's work.
He stayed until midnight to talk it out, not expecting
a solution would be offered, but only to pour his distress into an ear that sympathized and understood.

Another, a young woman who believed her "prince
had come," told her secret with radiant face and talked
over the plans for the days ahead. She had many and
perplexing problems to face before she pledged her
life to any man.

Then a father, whose son was afflicted with loco-
motor ataxia. The difficulties of living with his son

increased daily. He was quarrelsome and mean toward those whose early discipline he threw off and on whom now the burden of supporting him fell.

There were two, who but a few days before had plighted their troth, who came to share their new happiness and to counsel about life's future with their minister and friend. Sermons their minister had preached had led the young man to desire the work of the ministry. If he did accept the ministry as his life work, he had to quit his position with one of the great banks of the city. How should it be done?

Again, it is a poor distressed soul driven almost mad by brooding on a great doctrine of the Christian faith, and she is now a case for the psychiatrist. The preacher must work with her if this soul is to find healing and peace.

Then it is a lad at the end of his junior year in college. He must decide what his life work is to be. He wants advice and direction.

Now, after twenty-eight years, it is a man in a great city who discovers the pastor of his boyhood home is to preach in a church near by. He attends. Listening to the sermon for the day, his disturbed mind escapes its conflicts and he lives the former days over in memory. Infelicities and religious conflicts in his home are troubling him and he needs the help of a friend. He seeks out this pastor of his early years that Sunday afternoon. For two hours he pours out his heart to him. He has come in fear of what seems to lie before him. He returns restored in courage and with new confidence in the source from which help comes.

These are cases typical in many preacher's experience, great and small, when he becomes a confidant for those who need one in the time of storm. They vitalize the atmosphere of his hours of preparation in the "ministry of the Word." When he studies his Bible, mindful of human need, he finds in its teaching many a candle that throws light on human experience. Under God, he is privileged to turn this light upon the way of men and women who wait for the message he brings to them.

Then again the preacher has his own tribulations to endure which prepare him to understand and counsel others who walk the sorrowful way. I am reminded now of the experience of one who had an afflicted child. The disease was one which, for foolish reasons, families desire not to make known. Before two years went by, it became known that this sorrow was at the preacher's fireside, and seven families in that parish went to him to be comforted because of a similar affliction in their homes. Only two of these were known to the assistant visitor in that parish when that pastorate was begun. Somehow or other, the pain of that sorrow had got into the message of the preacher and also the grace with which he had learned to carry it. Men and women likewise afflicted came to talk of their sorrow and to learn how it might be borne.

It is for reasons bound up in such experiences that I say, if possible, have your study in your home. There is something in the environment of home, to which weary, burdened, sinful men and women can come and feel at rest when they want to lay bare the secrets of life. Out of such an environment reports do not seep and flow to the outside world.

There is much that can be said for a study in the church, or an office for consultation, especially in a great city, where multitudes are accustomed to professional interviews. In such places they feel the indifference of the public is some protection from observing eyes. But in the average parish of the country, the town, and the small city, the home is the best location for the study. It is where all the great sanctities of love, sympathy, understanding, and protection are housed. Where the preacher lives, there he can minister to needy folk.

Chapter XII

WHAT IS EFFECTIVE PREACHING?

Preaching is inseparably associated with the propagation of Christian truth. "The roots of Christian preaching lie far back of the Christian Era. They are stuck in the soil of the Old Testament and deeper even than that, in one common human heart."[1]

In the Old Testament we have a word, *bawsar* (Ps. 40: 9, Isa. 61: 1) translated in the Authorized version, *preached, to preach*—the root meaning of which is "to be cheerful," and which Moffatt translates, "told the good news." The whole verse as he translates it is, "Thou knowest, Eternal One, that openly I told the good news to our gathering; I kept not to myself thy saving help, but told aloud thy loyalty and aid, making no secret of thy love and faithfulness" (Ps. 40: 9). Then in Isa. 61: 1, "The Eternal; he inspires me, for the Eternal has consecrated me, and sent me with good news for wretched men, to heal the broken hearted, to tell prisoners they are free, to tell captives they are released," etc. There are two other Hebrew words meaning *to call out, to proclaim* (Neh. 6: 7), and *koheleth, an assembler* (Eccl. 1: 2) which are also suggestive of the function of preaching in the Old Testament times. Still another word used, *nabi*, "derived from a verb, *naba*, which is traced to a root signifying

157

to boil over or bubble up, and its passive form suggests that the speaker is moved by impulses over which he has not entire control."[2] Such words indicate to us that preaching did not begin with the Christian era. Preaching was a familiar incident in Old Testament times.

When we reach New Testament times we find several Greek words for preaching. We mention three. The first is *euaggelizo*—to proclaim good news; the second, *kerusso*—to speak as a herald the word of an ambassador;[3] the third, *prophates*, i.e., one who speaks of coming events, who speaks in public places, who speaks as the representative of another.[4] In such words there are indications of the changing character of the preacher's functioning. The early propagation of Christian truth was effected in the familiar talk, conversation, or discussion which individuals or groups of individuals had with each other. Then the process became more formal both in the preparation made for it and in the character of the audience to which the message was addressed. The vocabulary of the vocation was necessarily enlarged. When these preachers became the representatives of organized congregations, when stated occasions called for men to speak with adequate preparation, when the worship developed liturgically and the sermon became a part of that process, the vocabulary of the people interested became broader. When institutions arose set to the task of preparing men, new words also were required to indicate their task.

But such words were at hand, rooted in the history that had been made as well as the things they described. The word *homilia* among the Greeks signified *conversation, mutual talk,* or *familiar discussion.* Among the Romans *sermo* was the word. In the periods following when schools were organized especially to instruct men to prepare sermons and to preach them to public assemblies, another word came into existence. The word that fittingly described the whole of the process had already been suggested. This word was *homiletics,* derived from homily. It referred to the whole compendium of knowledge, the principles of learning involved and the instruction given. Homiletics designated the "science which treats of the nature, the classification, the analysis, the construction, and the composition of a sermon. More concisely, it is the science of that of which preaching is the *art* and a sermon is the product."[5]

The study of homiletics was early associated with the study of rhetoric and logic; but nowadays, when the completion of study leading to a B.A. degree is required of those who enter the theological seminary and courses leading to a theological degree, the department of homiletics often assumes that the subjects of rhetoric and logic have been studied preparatory to homiletics. Without such preparatory study the student is not equipped to take full advantage of the instruction in homiletics.

The preacher's task is to convey Christian truth to others by instruction, by narration, by illustration, by reasoning. If, for instance, it be by reasoning, he ought to be acquainted with the different kinds of argument available. The conclusion to be established must be presented to the mind of him who is conducting the argument and whose business it is to find proofs of the given proposition.[6] The object to be effected is to convince his hearer, who is ignorant of, or indifferent to, or unconvinced of the truth, of its importance or its validity. So, also, the hearer who is of contrary opinion.

Preaching is the utterance of divine truth with a view to the persuasion of the hearer to accept that truth, to incorporate it in his life, and give effect to it in his conduct and conversation.

Since preaching has become identified with organized Christianity, with definite relation to its forms of worship, the function of the preacher has been broadened "to represent Christianity as a religion, not as a science (but) religion incorporated and as manifesting itself in the church, to give expression to the experience of the common Christian life. This presupposes a congregation that shares this common experience in adequate measure with the preacher. Preaching is a part of the service of common worship, all the elements of which are testimony as to the reality of the inner Christian life. This gives preaching a distinct Christian character, and it must have a certain liturgical quality. The congregation cannot be treated as if wholly without religious life and experience and as if practically in pagan condition."[7]

With this brief statement of the history of our vocabulary and the inherent meaning of the preaching task, let us consider basic facts which describe effective preaching.

Effective preaching rests upon certain definite considerations which center in the preacher himself. We mention five such considerations:

1. *Effective preaching depends upon the preacher's knowledge and experience of the truth.* He may be able to quote long passages from the Bible or to locate

proof-texts in defense of some doctrine or creed and yet not *know* the truth. He may be able to talk well about the life and ministry of the Carpenter of Nazareth and yet never utter a phrase so that his utterance indicates he *knows Him.* A college president some years ago was in search of a Bible teacher and visited a young woman highly recommended. After a conference an hour and thirty minutes long he told her he did not believe she was fitted for the work because in that hour and a half she gave no indication that she knew Jesus, though she was well informed about Him. Her friends were sure he was mistaken and persuaded him to invite her to his staff. In less than six weeks he had to dismiss her, because she failed utterly to convince her associates in the college, both students and faculty, that she had any *experience* in the truth she was talking about. She never spoke of Jesus as one speaks of a friend with whom the tryst of love is kept.

"Truth through personality is our description of real preaching," says Phillips Brooks. "The truth must come really through the person, not merely over his lips, not merely into his understanding and out through his pen. It must come through his character, his affections, his whole intellectual and moral being."[8] There is a difference in the language of the man who has worked out his problems in the laboratory and the man whose talk is only out of what he has read about it. There is authority in the words, "We know we have passed from death unto life, because we love the brethren," as they fall from the lips of a man who loves the brethren in contrast with the man who can only repeat the words. The one has experience in loving men; the other has not. This experience of the gospel truth is fundamental to success in preaching. "For surely we are going to lay it down as our first axiom, never to be forgotten, that we are not to be mere shadows, and pale reflexions of anyone else, however distinguished, but mean to come to God on our own feet, and think Him out as best we can in our own poor human fashion with our own minds, to express in the way natural to us what we ourselves have found from our own first hand reading and experience."[9]

2. *Effective preaching will depend upon the development and enrichment of the preacher's personality.* We shall return to this subject in Chapter XV. We now call attention to it briefly by saying, development and enrichment of personality is attained by the man who works diligently, continually, consistently at his task of preparation; who disciplines himself, his instincts, his tendencies, in this or that direction; who "brings his body into subjection"; who seeks the companionship of lofty souls and takes time to commune with God and his own soul. No factor bulks larger in all vocations of life than the factor of personality, even though there is so little agreement among the learned as to just what is personality. Though differing in quality and magnitude in different individuals, personality is marked by the power to illuminate, vitalize, and transform whatever passes through it. It gives color and form, impact and force, to the utterance of the preacher. The development and enrichment of personality was one of the remarkable attainments in the history of Abraham Lincoln as noted by those who associated with him in the early history of Illinois. Here, also, is the secret of power for the preacher: let him study and mark the personality values in all biographies he

reads; then endeavor to incorporate the best values in his own life.

3. *Efficient preaching depends upon the gift for expression.* The preacher must know and have the ability to state what he knows. It matters not how opulent he may be in ideas. Ideas are valuable only when expressed in clear, correct, and vital speech. A man may be diligent and skilful in digging down to the roots of words he finds in the Scripture. He may be gifted in comprehending the sweep of thought expressed by the authors he reads. But unless he can find words to express that thought to the simple as well as the learned who want to know, he will not be efficient in the transference to others of what he has gained in reading. He may become a learned preacher; but he will not be an efficient one. It is well to remember ideas must not only be incorporated in words but words must also be so joined one to the other as to give acceptable expression to the ideas. Words are the vehicles of ideas; but the vehicle must be able to make its way and carry its load if it is to be useful to men. One of the saddest of comments to be made about preachers is often uttered—"He is a good man, but he can't preach." It indicates, oftentimes, for example, such a man has not gained a vocabulary, which is possible to every man who sets himself to get it. Let such a man record each new word that comes to his attention, give earnest study to its origin and history, and find early occasion in conversation, writing, or utterance to use it. Thus a vocabulary will be gained in due time to express his ideas. He will be able to speak in such a way that the simple as well as the wise will attend to what he says.

4. *Then, again, efficient preaching depends upon the*

preacher's acquaintance with the Word of God, the Scriptures of the Old and New Testaments. One of the regrettable things that has happened to preachers in America is their neglect of the Bible and the consequent result that has followed: i.e., the decline and death of Biblical preaching. Our preachers do not deal with great Biblical themes. They are too much concerned with current problems. The timeless elements of preaching presented in the Bible have been neglected for the passing interests of time. The magazines and newspapers are taking care of these matters; and when ministers neglect their Bibles for current events, the subjects the preacher should present for the thoughtful consideration of men, such as God, Jesus Christ, the Holy Spirit, the forgiveness of sins, righteousness that exalteth a nation, peace, which the heart of man longs for, faith, hope, immortality, prayer, victory over sin, and other great subjects which the people need, have no one responsible for their proclamation.

It is the preacher's duty to proclaim these as they are presented in the revelation of God to men. The Bible is a compendium of such truth. It is an Old Book. But it is the "epitome of history." The preacher can leave other things to other men. He must preach the message of God to men. There is no source upon which the preacher can draw so rich and authoritative in what is eternally significant to the race as the Bible presents to the man who knows his Book. I have just finished a glance at the latest number of a sermon magazine, and I venture to say the most interesting and effective sermon in that number is the sermon of a young man who speaks on "The Humility of God" —an exposition of that marvelous scene in the Gospel of John when Jesus washed the disciples' feet. In this exposition, the preacher revealed his discovery of the human and divine values in the Bible. America, particularly, needs more preaching like that. When one attends to the message of such a sermon to a generation that has lost its way, he gets a new vision of the glory of a life that is "hid with Christ in God." He gets strength to live valiantly in his own day.

5. *Again, efficient preaching will depend upon the preacher's love for his fellow-men.* In a world that is in deadly conflict, when nations are being led by men who tell them that "by war alone can nations fulfill their destiny," that "war alone brings up to its highest tension all human energy and places the stamp of nobility on the peoples who have the courage to meet it," we know the power of the beast is at work. Such utterances alone have the stamp of the beast upon them. When salesmen of great munitions manufacturing corporations speak of their employment as a "hell of a business," surely the time has come for preachers to cry aloud in the streets the gospel of love and peace on earth, good will among men.

There is nothing for which the world is in such need as love. "Love thinketh no evil, rejoiceth not in iniquity but rejoiceth in the truth, beareth all things, believeth all things, hopeth all things, endureth all things, love never faileth." It is the language all men, from the least unto the greatest, can understand. They go up and down the highways, the streets, and alleys of our great cities, looking for those who can speak a word of comfort, sympathy, love, and too often find them not. But when they do find men who have this accent in their preaching, they hearken to and embrace

them. "Comfort ye, comfort ye my people, saith your
God." That is the word of the ancient prophet. That
is the word for the modern prophet to a generation
that is distressed. Men who can speak to the heart
of mankind and can dry the tears of those who weep,
who can guide the wayward and strengthen the weak,
these are the men who can interpret God to the world.
Such are efficient preachers.

WHAT IS A SERMON?

There are many definitions. Dr. Herrick Johnson
said, "a sermon is a formal religious discourse founded
upon the Word of God, designed to save men."[10]   In
his *Theory of Preaching*, Austin Phelps says, "The
sermon is an oral address to the popular mind, on
a religious truth contained in the Scriptures and
elaborately treated with a view to persuasion."[11] We
would say, a sermon is a religious discourse founded
on the Word of God designed to secure the action of
the will toward Christ-likeness in the individual and
in his social relations. If several definitions be examined as given by teachers of homiletics, they will
be found to be agreed in several particulars: (1) The
sermon is a public discourse (2) founded upon the
Word of God (3) for a particular and direct purpose
(4) usually in connection with public worship, (5)
addressed to the popular mind.

The sermon is not, therefore, an abstruse, philosophical, lengthy treatment of a given theme addressed
to learned intellectuals of a congregation or community. If the preacher be called upon to speak to
the learned, let him remember to speak with simplicity
and directness, even as he would speak to any group

or assembly. When he appeals to the reason, let him remember the reason is to be respected. But it is not the citadel to be taken. It is the will and the imagination he is to capture. It is the will he is to move. Let him, therefore, take account of those considerations upon which the whole human race is moved to courses of action. "The true end of preaching," cautioned Susanna Wesley when writing to her son, "is to mend men's lives and not to fill their heads with unprofitable speculations."[12] Yes, and we might add, it is not to deal in any fashion with mere speculations, however profitable. It is to proclaim a revelation. If men, hearing it, indulge in speculations and end with that, the end for which the sermon should be prepared has not been attained.

It is well to distinguish between the sermon and the lecture. A lecture treats a subject for the primary purpose of informing the mind, for the improvement of the intelligence, either as to the minutiae of the subject matter or its broad implications. The treatment may be learned dullness to the popular mind, yet satisfy all the inherent demands of a true lecture. The lecturer may maintain an attitude of indifference toward his hearers, acceptance or rejection of his utterances. His purpose in lecturing is to inform and not to persuade or enlist. If his lecture informs and enlists, then he has attained a success that is desirable and pleasing; but both achievements are not required of him for efficient lecturing. As a lecturer, too great zeal for enlistments may compromise his effectiveness. He becomes a propagandist and is in danger of losing the confidence of his audience that he has that fine regard for facts and their validity, which is the obligation of the teacher and instructor of men's minds.

But a sermon, while it must be true to the facts and loyal to the truth, is not primarily to inform the mind, but to move the hearer to change his course. In Christian countries, it is especially the case of a man speaking to people who already know the truth, who may be informed of the facts of the gospel history, often more accurately and extensively than the preacher who brings the sermon. In such a case it is the primary duty of the preacher to persuade men, to lead them to do and be what they know they ought to *do* and *be*. He should *preach for a verdict*, in accordance with the truth of revelation in Christ Jesus.

Again it is well to remember the differences between the sermon and the essay. An essay is defined as "a literary composition, analytical or interpretative in dealing with its subject from a more or less limited or personal standpoint and permitting a considerable freedom of style and method."[13] It is usually a short treatise that may be easily and completely read at one sitting. The essay is the expression of personal opinion offered to its hearers. It reveals the mind of the writer upon the subject treated. The hearer is privileged to take or leave what is offered. It may be judged on its literary merits, on the value of the wisdom or knowledge of the author indicated therein. It seldom becomes the vehicle of any urgency of conviction. The absence of such urgency does not destroy its value. The essay is only obligated to present, in the best form possible, the opinions or judgments or thoughts of the writer, and in a manner acceptable or pleasing to those for whom it has been prepared.

The sermon, on the other hand, brings the message

of a commissioned representative. The heart of the message is the mind of "Another,"[14] as Dr. Buttrick expresses it. The preacher's obligation is to be faithful to that "Another." Personal opinions, views, theories, interpretations, or whatever may be an expression of himself must be brought into subjection to the One whom he represents. He is a herald, a witness, an announcer, whose whole duty is discharged in getting before his auditor the message committed to him and in getting action upon it. This is the concept of his task that must get into the consciousness and control of the preacher. The legitimacy, value, and authority of his utterance is in the fact and in his right to say, "I believe I have the mind of Christ in saying what I say to you."

The orator has no such limitations, if this may be described as a limitation. He may gain much if he has been commissioned. Henry Ward Beecher felt he spoke in England as the representative of the people and the government of the United States in 1863. The orator may desire to persuade men. If he does so desire he may in that measure approach a likeness to the preacher. Preachers, in the power of their speech, or the expression of their message, may become like the orator. That likeness will be in the clarity, beauty, and force with which they express their truth; in the wisdom and skill they display in the selection of their arguments; in the grace and charm with which they arrange their subject matter; or in the vision, the work of their constructive imagination, in building up great periods of thought and expression, for orators are chiefly concerned with these qualities being found in their production. These qualities are not the first consideration of the true preacher on any occasion that he preaches. These are accidental in preaching elements. If the preacher by warmth and vividness, grace and passion, expresses his message in grand style and winning words, it is well. It is *not necessary*, so to speak. To be counted worthy or efficient, he is required to speak faithfully the message given him, whether men "hear or forbear."

The orator is usually concerned to speak pleasingly. He may have a great cause or a great occasion to celebrate. He gives voice to the multitude he addresses and who are like-minded with himself. He speaks convincingly, perhaps, but the power of it is in the mastery of his style, the excellence of his personality or his cause. In the case of the preacher, all the excellencies of the orator may be found, but the supreme excellence is in the truth he presents, the experience of the truth he proclaims, and in his fidelity to his commission. But he is not required by his commission to please. His confidence lies in the assurance that the Spirit of God is speaking through him. Whether men hear, or whether they forbear to hear, he must be able to say, "Not unto us, O Lord, not unto us, but unto Thee be the glory, dominion, and power, now and forevermore."

Let us conclude then, *Effective Preaching* is not a secret of technique alone. It is the gift of the Holy Spirit. He finds a personality through whom he can express the mind of God and baptizes him with the power of utterance.

The usefulness of such a personality lies in part in his *preparation for the Holy Spirit's use*. This is the reason he should possess the principles and the technique of sermon building. These possessions consecrated in him unto the task of preparing his sermon and himself for the Holy Spirit's use will make him efficient. This seems to be a sufficient "apology" for homiletic instruction and preparation in a theological seminary, or in whatever place a man is found *who is dedicated to the Master's use.*

CHAPTER XIII

THE WARRANT FOR PREACHING

CRITICISM of preachers and their preaching is recorded in every century. In his *Ambassadors of God,* Dr. S. Parkes Cadman has a chapter on "Modern Attitude toward Preaching," in which he reminds us, "Nor is there very much which is new in the prejudices and misapprehensions unfavorable to your calling. In reviewing such matters, many of which are of the commonest observation, you do not navigate uncharted waters dangerously rife with reef and shoal, in which there are no openings, no broad expanse, for the fullest exercise of the preaching office."[1]

The examination of such a chart as Dr. Cadman's fruitful imagination suggests will reveal a difference in the nature and occasions of these criticisms in the various periods observed. It will reveal the ebb and flow of their tides—now full, then shallow, as though about to run out. At one time their sweep is violent and deadly in character, crushing the heart of the preacher and his utterances; then, again, their effects are impotent and weak, making no impression upon the preacher.

In some periods the atmosphere of social, intellectual, political life is cold and indifferent. Preachers and preaching have been deemed not of sufficient importance to merit critical attention. The opposition assuming preachers were without warrant, that preaching was an impertinence, with haughty superiority, has ignored the preacher and his message as something that did not count, beneath the attention of intelligent and achieving men. Preaching was a profession no longer needed in the world's work, having been superseded by more effective instruments of expression—even as the ancient reaper's sickle and cradle have been superseded by the harvesting machines in the fields of grain.

There is a difference in the homiletic lectures and essays of, let us say, the middle quarter of the nineteenth century and that since the closing of the last quarter and the opening third of the twentieth century. In the first period there is the absence of awareness of serious criticism of preaching. Homiletic lectures, sermons, and essays moved in a world that accepted preaching as one of the learned professions. By the time we approach the threshold of the twentieth century a change has taken place. We begin to hear the apologetic note in defense of preaching. It indicates the critical process has been already felt and some recognition of its strictures is expressed, if in nothing more than the title of a book. So all the way from *Modern Criticism and the Preaching of the Old Testament,* by Dr. George Adam Smith (1901) down to *Jesus came Preaching,* by Dr. George A. Buttrick (1931), we feel the reaction to the critical current of the hour.

A leaflet[2] was recently printed by a society organized for the purpose of "elevating the ministerial profession in dignity and quality and giving it a place of deserved influence in society." It indicates the em-

phasis of current criticism on at least two points—
"quality" and "influence." According to this publication, contrary to an aged claim and recognition, the
ministry is not a learned profession (with data and per-
centages to prove it). Instead of improving, the preaching situation rapidly grows worse as to quality. And
most arresting, also, is the fact, that, interest in effecting
the proper changes is difficult to arouse. There are
many reasons, therefore, indicating it is well for a man
who expects to preach or who is already preaching to
give heed, not only as an answer to the challenge as
to his right to preach but also as an incentive to improvement in personality and the practice of his art.
For "the question of the ultimate for mankind is the
greatest of all the questions which meet the west, since
the (Roman) Catholic Church lost its place in the
sixteenth century, and since criticism no longer allows
the Bible to occupy that place. Yet the Gospel of the
future must come with the note of authority. The
first duty of every soul is to find not its freedom, but
its Master."[3]

I. *We find the warrant for preaching in the example
of Jesus Christ.* 1. Christ, Himself, "came preaching."
"Now after that John was put in prison, Jesus came into
Galilee, preaching the gospel of the kingdom of God,
and saying, the time is fulfilled, and the kingdom of
God is at hand: repent ye, and believe the gospel"
(Mark 1:14-15). Luke, in the fourth chapter and
eighteenth verse, gives another instance in which there
is a description of His manner and a hint of His message. He also further states, "And it came to pass
afterward, that he went throughout every city and vil-

lage, preaching and shewing the glad tidings of the kingdom of God" (Luke 8:1).

The note of authority was in His preaching. This
authority is accounted for in two factors of the bio-
graphic narratives: 1. The quality of His personality.
2. His actual accomplishments. Matthew observes this
(7: 28-29), the word used indicating something of the
effect this authority had upon those who heard. Luke,
also, again notes that He spoke with charming effects—
"winning words fell from His lips" (Luke 4: 22) as
Dr. Goodspeed's translation has it.[4] He also spoke encouragingly, "showing the glad tidings" (Luke 8:1).
Such was the example Jesus gave us for preaching.

II. *Jesus commissioned other men to preach.* Preaching is the Christ-appointed means for the propagation
of the gospel. Dr. Arthur Hoyt observes[5]: "Wherever
in the New Testament the call to the ministry is spoken
of, preaching is the point made emphatic." When He
had equipped the Twelve with the matchless enkindling
of their personalities, which His personality and word
gave to them, He sent them forth, saying, "And as ye
go, preach, saying, The kingdom of heaven is at hand"
(Matt. 10: 7). These twelve men accompanied Jesus
wherever He went until the day of His crucifixion.
After His resurrection from the dead, He commissioned
them to carry on the work He had begun and of which
they had been witnesses.

If we examine the recorded utterances of these men,
we cannot escape the consciousness of authority they
possessed and that carries over to us as we read their
words. They are free from the timidity which uncertainty or fear begets. They are free from bluster or
bluff in their utterance. They are under the spell of a

great conviction, awakened in men who have come to grips with vital experience of the truth. They proclaim what is "most surely believed amongst" them. They say what they know God has commanded them. Whether men hear or forbear to believe is not the great matter. That is the responsibility of the hearer. If they refuse to hear, these commissioned men go on to the next village, uttering their message as men who are primarily responsible to Him who gave them their commission. And in the last appearance of Jesus and His disciples, it is recorded the principal word He left with them was to go into all the world and preach the gospel (Matt. 28: 19-20; Mark 16: 15; Luke 24: 47).

In obedience to this command, the disciples did that. They spoke with authority, as the record shows. Note the word of authority with which Peter spoke on the day of Pentecost (Acts 2: 14): "Ye men of Judea, and all ye that dwell at Jerusalem, be this known unto you, and hearken to my words" (2: 22). Again, "Ye men of Israel, hear these words" (3: 12-26). And as he stood before the authorities as recorded in Acts 4: 20, he declared, "We cannot but speak the things which we have seen and heard." They were men under authority who spoke with authority.

III. *The warrant for preaching is indicated in the teaching and experience of Paul.*

Paul speaks with the conviction of a commissioned man. It is indicated in all his Epistles and in every utterance. He generally begins his Epistles by declaring in some form of speech that he was the appointed messenger of Christ. He speaks in I Cor. 1: 1, "Called to be an apostle." II Cor. 1: 1: "An apostle of Jesus Christ." Gal. 1: 1: "Paul, an apostle, not of men, neither by man, but by Jesus Christ, and God the Father." He was ready and unashamed to preach. Rom. 1: 15: "I am ready to preach." He was convinced preaching is the divine method for redeeming the world (Rom. 10:13-15; I Cor. 1:21). Preaching was his unescapable duty. "Though I preach the gospel, I have nothing to glory of; woe is me if I preach not the gospel." "I cannot help doing it" (Goodspeed). The gravity of Paul's view is indicated in his letter to Timothy (II Tim. 4: 1-5). He was in the sight of God. He urges him to constant fidelity and indicates the comprehensive character of the task to convince, to reprove, to exhort with patience and longsuffering, and to teach.

In splendid succession, from that day to this, men have preached because necessity was laid upon them. These men could not help doing it. There was a drive from within. They had a message. They wanted to preach, to tell what God had done for their souls. They not only had a message; the message had them.

To recall Dr. Buttrick's statement mentioned in the last chapter, "Preaching is grounded in that awareness of Another. Christian preaching is rooted in the persuasive faith and piercing conviction that in Christ that Other has made known His love and will for mankind."[6] They must make known what He had done.

IV. *The warrant for preaching, then, rises out of the preacher's Christian experience.* The man who has met Christ as his personal Savior has the consciousness that he has come in contact with reality. It cannot be successfully denied that Jesus Christ is an historical figure. The process of examination of the history of His times, and the proofs of His existence, the study of the records of His life and action handed down to us, have been as thorough and searching as friends and foe could make it. The flood of publicity and criticism, constructive and destructive, has beat upon His historical presence in the world, has exposed every defect in the record, and illuminated every item of His claim. The battle has raged about this standard, its accompaniments and associations, with the result of settling the historical fact of Jesus of Nazareth, who was called Christ, beyond doubt and destruction. No historical personage is more certainly a factor in the history and march of the world than Jesus called the Christ.

A similar examination and, in conjunction with this, examination of *Him* as an historical fact, should be applied to His teaching. While there are different schools of interpretation, the solidity of His teaching is impregnable. He did live. He did teach. He wrought and suffered and died. These facts cannot be overthrown. They are established.

Whatever divisions may exist among believers have arisen in the different understandings men have of the significance of the words used, or the implication of His utterance in its broad and historical application. Some of these differences and those most difficult to reconcile have grown out of the philosophical postulates with which men have approached the Gospel content and the witness of believers. Men who have begun their study or who have, in the process, assumed the impossibility of the miracle or the improbability of the "facts" as set forth, necessarily deny the more simple believer's testimony and interpretation as recorded. If they start with the assumption that miracles do not happen, that all historical and discoverable data occur in conformity with principles embedded in the very constitution of the universe, from which there is no variation, in which there can be no variableness except toward chaos and destruction, then they are certain to find the Gospel narratives not dependable as historical documents and the teaching attributed to Jesus about Himself as worshipful enthusiasms or evidences of mythological beliefs and superstitions. When such persons confront those records that are undeniable, they must interpret them in such a way as to exclude the miraculous.

The situation for such intellectuals (for only such are in this group), is, however, embarrassing, because Jesus, called the Christ, must be explained, as well as the effects that have been set in motion by His presence.

To begin with the utterances of Jesus are incomparable, not only in their simplicity of form but in their substance. "No man ever spake as this man spake," was the judgment of His contemporaries; and that is the judgment of the centuries succeeding them.

In the second place, the association of simple, unlearned, uninfluential fishermen and taxgatherers, also schooled and capable thinkers with Jesus Christ, telling their story, giving their witness, revealing the implications of Jesus Christ's profound utterances, has put them in the focused perspective of world thought and esteem. By virtue of their Christo-centric interest, conviction, utterance, and supreme devotion to Him, Jesus Christ has made those men immortals. But the effect of this Jesus, called Christ in history, is also to be accounted for. If Jesus were only a man, with a larger possession of divinity than any before, during, or since His time, that would be something arresting from every side on which man finds himself. But it is also an equally arresting fact that whenever men met Him and wherever and whenever they have heard about Him and have decided to venture in faith upon His teaching, they have come to an experience of reality. Jesus is to such men not an historical figure but a *contemporary* personage. They can keep tryst with Him. They can co-operate with Him. They can know the healing, comforting ministry of His Presence in the time of need and feel the vitalizing power of strength they lack for the day of struggle and combat. From Paul's day of assertion of this, men and women have been able to attempt the impossible and accomplish it "through Him who strengtheneth me." Such men and women do not depend alone upon an historical figure, who lived humbly, wrought righteously, and died valiantly. They depend on Him who conquered Death, Who rose again from the dead, Who fulfills His promise to be with His loved ones even unto the end of the ages.

It is out of such an experience preaching springs. When a man comes to such fulness of life, he passes beyond the reach of the arrows of doubt and anxiety as to the authenticity of literature. He knows it is authentic because he has made the venture of faith that it is true and has found reality. Such a man says, "I know Him in whom I have believed."

It is possible now to see implications and understand the real significance of the words and phrases and teachings utterly beyond the range of a life that has not made this adventure. This New Testament record has caught at the center of individual personality. It has become the fountain of life that has blessed him with a life most abundant. This truth has "gripped him at the vitals."

When such a man wants to preach he not only has a message but the message has him. He sees the world-need of this message and when such a man speaks to that world, whatever defects there may be in his utterance, the presence of God and the authority of His presence in the personality of this preacher will be speaking.

V. That preaching is the Christ-appointed means for propagating the gospel and for bringing men to Christ and a saving knowledge of the truth, is *evident in the direct results of preaching*.

1. The record of preaching in the New Testament begins with John the Baptist (Matt. 3: 5-6). It is modestly stated that there "went out to him Jerusalem, and all Judea, and all the region round about Jordan, and were baptized of him in Jordan, confessing their sins." John's preaching was courageous, searching, denunciatory, and challenging. In consequence, he lost his head. He preached as he was commissioned and valiantly paid for it with his life. But he did not lack an audience nor converts.

On the Day of Pentecost, Peter preached, as commissioned, basing his message on the fulfillment of God's promised outpouring of His Spirit as given in prophecy and fulfilled in history and particularly in the person of Jesus Christ. As a result, "they that gladly received his word were baptized: and the same day there were added unto them about three thousand souls." He continued in this method of witnessing, instructing, and exhorting until his martyrdom.

There followed in this line the Apostles, Barnabas, John, Mark, Paul, and Timothy, and as a result the Christian church was increased until these men had carried the gospel and won converts not only throughout Palestine but also in numerous cities of Asia Minor, Macedonia, Greece, and the Roman Empire. Paul addressed his letters to them in Rome, Corinth, Ephesus, Philippi, Colosse, and Thessalonica. Peter sent epistles to the elect according to the foreknowledge of God in Pontus, Galatia, Cappadocia, Asia, and Bythynia. And John addressed his apocalyptic-vision letter to "the seven churches which are in Asia" (Rev. 1: 4). So that, in the few short years of a lifetime and before the close of the first Christian century, these preachers and their colaborers had preached the gospel and won converts in many cities and countries of the western and near east world. The genuineness of this work is witnessed to in the *koinonia,* or brotherhood, which was set up, and in the harmony and happiness, the service and sacrifice, that described them.

The valiancy and faithfulness of their preaching was also witnessed to in the persecutions they endured. All men did not yield themselves. Some mocked. Oppositions were raised, and they were hounded in various places, a testimony of their faithfulness to their commission. They built a church that has never been stamped out. We can, therefore, say the historic church was developed by preaching as by no other means.

Since that, faithful preachers have been found in every age who have heard the call and proclaimed the truth of the revelation of God in Jesus Christ. Great revival movements in Europe, Britain, and America have been carried forward by preachers. The Protestant Reformation in the sixteenth century, the Methodist revival in the eighteenth, and the preaching and revivals of the nineteenth century, have continued to promulgate the truth until now there are millions throughout the world who have heard the good news from the lips of men touched by the Holy Spirit, witnessing to the "power of God unto salvation to everyone that believeth."

VI. Probably the conviction of the church was never so clear or so universally held as at this present hour that *the perpetuation and vigor of the spiritual life of God's people is dependent upon gospel preaching.* The various historic denominations have been awakened to the importance of such preaching to a degree unheard of in previous generations. Great organized movements have been set in motion in preaching missions to effect this. Men and women skilled in the utterance and application of this gospel are being selected and sent out annually to great centers of population, to urban and rural districts, to preach the cardinal truths of that gospel and to support the work of the ministry. "Preaching has ever been the chief means of propagating our faith," said a great Christian editor. "The prophets of the Old Testament were great preachers. Jesus came preaching and sent His disciples to preach. There are other means, important in their place, especially the Bible and Christian literature, but preaching has a directness and power of appeal that the printed page does not have. It is the expression and imparting of the very soul of the preacher and enters into the soul of the hearer with subtle and captivating power. It sends truth as a living stream into the minds and hearts of the audience and may insensibly do its work even against the prejudice and opposition of the hearers. For this reason it cannot be displaced by any other means, even by radio. The

power of the Protestant churches has been in their
pulpits and not in the visible appeals of the forms of
worship, vital and powerful as these are." "Rightly
understood," said another, a great prophet of the last
forty years, "mankind lives and grows on great sermons, and in no other way."[8]

Preaching has enlisted the choicest personalities of
all ages in this great task of the perpetuation and vigor
of God's people: Clement of Rome (in the first century), Justin Martyr, of the second century, Origen and
Cyprian, of the second and third century, Basil and
Augustine of the fourth, Chrysostom at the close of the
fourth and opening of the fifth, Gregory I, in the
sixth, Bede in the seventh and eighth, Anschar in the
ninth, Adelbert in the tenth, Peter the Hermit in the
eleventh, Bernard in the eleventh and twelfth, Francis
of Assisi in the twelfth and thirteenth, Bonaventura in
the thirteenth, Bernardino of Sienna in the fourteenth
and fifteenth, Luther in the fifteenth and sixteenth, with
a noble company of preachers in the Reformation movement—Zwingli, Calvin, John Knox, Hugh Latimer, John
Wesley, and George Whitefield, on down to the men
in this land—Edwards, Lyman Beecher, Charles Finney,
Bushnell, Brooks, Henry Ward Beecher, Stoors, to men
of our present day. This noble succession has stood
up and preached. They have proclaimed the unsearchable riches of Christ. Moral and religious giants, men
of social passion and political insight, men of missionary zeal and utterance, have always been found
to speak the truth as it is in Christ. In consequence,
the church has never ceased to look for and listen to
them. Without such utterance, the church could not
have continued.

VII. *Ministering in the pulpit is a noble and practical service.* The forces of evil have witnessed to their fear of preachers. In one of the great campaigns against the liquor traffic in this country some years ago, they exhorted their cohorts through the columns of their press to "keep the preachers out of this fight." Preachers are dangerous men to workers of iniquity. Such men as Dr. George Truett, Dr. Mark Matthews, Dr. J. Valdemar Moldenhauer, Dr. Walter Maier, the late Dr. John VanderMeulen, and many others living and dead, could be named as faithful prophets of this generation who have lifted up their voices against corruption in government, against war, child labor, corrupt politicians, selfish business and industry, and all the other evils to which the nation and the world are addicted. They are representative of preachers in the nation who struggle for a better society and a righteous humanity.

There is no place throughout our land where these preachers do not go to comfort the bereaved and sick, to support the dying, to bless little children. Wherever strong men faint and youths grow weary, these messengers of the lowly Jesus, these preachers are there to be a stand-by and friend, a shelter in the time of storm. Their ministrations of mercy do not have to be paid for in dollars and cents. They serve where human need calls.

Not long since a minister returned to his former parish in a great city to celebrate the anniversary of a church's organization. Many testimonies of affection were given to him by people who remembered his ministry of love. Among those was a young business man who told him his gratitude for a sermon he preached. Said he to the minister, "I want you to know that sermon has been one of the constructive forces of my life. I can give you the text and the outline of what you said on that occasion. I have never had the opportunity to tell you before, how much what you said has meant to me; so I wanted to tell you now." It was nearly twenty-one years before that word of gratitude was spoken in the ears of that minister. But the word had been spoken, and a lad, hearing, had walked under the influence of that word to an established reputation for integrity and success in the business world.

Preachers deal with problems that neither science nor philosophy, medicine, law, or instruments of education touch with a healing hand as does the ministry from the pulpit. These messengers of mercy, human and divine, drop seeds of truth in the soil of the heart and mind that germinate and spring up, blossom and bear fruit in times and places unknown to any person except the God who sent them and the souls that received the word He sent.

God has purposed that His word be mediated through an intelligent and vibrant personality experienced in this truth who is able to utter it to those who can be reached in no other way but who may be reached through the listening ear. "How shall they believe in Him of whom they have not heard? and how shall they hear without a preacher? and how shall they preach except they be sent?" The problem as thus stated is not one of missionary support with ample finances. It is a question as to the authorization of any man with such a message. This message is one no man could conceive, no man can impart, no man can validate.

This message is about God. What man knoweth the mind of God that he should declare it? He cannot declare the mind of any man (except his own), until that man has made known his mind and commissioned the preacher to speak it. So this preacher, having the mind of God to proclaim, first has it from God, in the center of his own being, awakening, transforming, redeeming the man, and sending him forth to a task the world calls foolishness but which, when performed, becomes the power of God to every other soul believing.

VIII. This brings us to the final warrant to be considered—*the call to the gospel ministry*. With most men, especially of the older schools, this is the distinction of preaching and that which sets it off from all other professions and guilds in which men employ their days. But there have been those who have taken another view. These have held the distinction of the ministry lies, not in the fact of a call, but in the purpose and the nature of the task to which the preacher is called. He is called of God to handle the message of God and to seek the saving of men. Such a call, therefore, differs in the content of the message, which is the revelation of God's will toward men, His incomparable love expressed in Jesus Christ—long-suffering, forgiving, merciful. It differs also in the fact a man is not seeking anything for himself, but the salvation of others. It requires the utter surrender of himself to God to be used for the great task upon which he is sent.

The man who has such a call must not only have the experience of such salvation, but he must have the ability to tell of it to others. He must be ready to prepare himself for that task. God does, as Dr. F. B.

Meyer said, "occasionally save by ram's horns; but more frequently He chooses the silver trumpet." The call to preach will, therefore, demand of a man that he secure the best possible preparation of himself in the use of those talents which are involved in the understanding and utterance of the truth.

In the second place it will involve his interest in people and the development of the social faculties. He must enter into the lives of other people, sympathize with them, be valiant in their interests and in the effort to understand their needs and be described by a willingness to meet them. If a man is not thus minded, if he does not love people, it is safe to say he is probably called to some other work.

In such a call comes the readiness of a man to be used wherever God may direct him to labor. If the love of power is in the blood of all the churches, as "Dick" Shepard intimates,[9] it is probably advisable that every young man considering the gospel ministry should examine himself to see if there be in him any unworthy ambition in seeking such an office and *to be rid of it,* if found. While there may be in some far greater fitness to serve in a particular field, that is a matter to be left to providential direction. Few men (as was George W. Truett) are "prayed into the ministry" by a congregation that observes their fitness and needs their services, but multitudes of men have been made conscious of the world's need of the gospel by this means and have been made eager to proclaim this gospel to that needy world.

Again, there comes to many men the consciousness of a direction to this glorious task for which they are qualified by nature and prepared by education. The very "stones of the field" seem to be leagued to lead them into that ministry.

The home in which they are born and brought up, the atmosphere of dominant interests, the environment of social and spiritual associations, the resources provided and necessary to their preparation and making it available, all unite to call them forth to take up this work. Such a man must have a passion for moral and spiritual values, and this he may have gained by inheritance as well as by acquirement. "For this work," Henry Ward Beecher reminds us, "you must have a vigorous life in you, and must be in earnest. Man cannot give it to you, books cannot give it to you, and even knowledge cannot give it to you. It only comes from Christ; it is by union with Him that you get this new force. And with Christ in your soul you will succeed in catching men. This union with God is the only true manhood for you, and the only true manhood for the manhood around you, and you must catch them and win them to it. So much then is determined—that you are to be fishers of men."[10]

CHAPTER XIV

THE PREPARATION OF THE PREACHER (I)

THERE are three distinct concerns that ought to engage the preacher in preparation for meeting his audience on the next Sunday.

I. *First is the preparation of his mind for the work.* The subject upon which he is to speak must be decided upon. The longer he has been thinking about it the better. The statement made by Henry Ward Beecher and some other masters that they kept five or six subjects constantly before them, which they could take up the last of the week and "feel" and see which was the ripest and most nearly ready for presentation is rather discouraging to a tyro, who does not have even one that seems ready. Happy the beginner who has been hard at work on his Bible and who is aware of the real problems of his people. Such a man usually feels the importance of something that must not be put off or that can be appropriately considered *now.*

Every preacher should realize the fact that God is speaking to men in revelation and in the present movements of life. The two must get their due proportion of consideration and presentation. The presentation of the message of revelation as an historical matter, unrelated to the work-a-day world in which people live, does not reach the will of earnest, active people. If revelation is a thing of the past, having no vital meaning for the living present, then it might just as well be wrapped in the grave-clothes of antiquity and buried. And if God is not speaking to us now, He has left us to ourselves, and we are in a sad plight. But every earnest, vibrant soul who has been called to preach knows the Word of God is living, vital, contemporaneous. The preacher who has devoted himself to understanding his Bible, his times, and the people with whom he lives, will by due meditation find his mind and heart filling with something to preach for which occasions are not numerous enough to present all he has to present.

Now that he has settled on what to preach, let him set to work to prepare his message. The development of what Dr. Herrick Johnson called "the homiletic bias" is the development of the power of the mind for preaching material and the habit of properly arranging it for climactic effect to impress the hearer with its values. The great orator observes and studies to attain the value of climax in public utterance and so also should the preacher. Develop, therefore, the gift of seeing the homiletic value of everything brought to your attention. Let it be grist to your mill. Your success will depend on your diligence in reading, your habit of meditation upon what you read, and the contact you make with people and with God. These are initial steps in gathering material for your message. It has a tremendously vitalizing effect upon the memory, as well as all faculties of the mind, and enables you to remember such values when the time for their use has come.

If you find your ability is sluggish or weak, then

the installation of devices for collecting and filing such material may be helpful. The process of filing this material which reading, conversation, or other contacts afford, develops in some men a mental habit of great value. When they master the method and do the work of putting the material away, they at least may remember where to get what they have and what they want and can resort to their treasury. Of course such persons must engage in the process of gathering materials. But they can never hope to compete with him who, having it in his memory, has it already at his mental finger tips, like a Moody, a Spurgeon, a Truett, or a Campbell Morgan.

Sermons come out of experience. By this I do not mean mental history measured by length of years, but the mental heat and vital living in the hour of every transaction in life. It is earnestness in living, honesty and sincerity in living, thoughtfulness and awareness in all the events of the day. The whole of a man's past is the treasury upon which such preachers draw. One cannot forget Mr. Webster's answer when asked how long it took him to prepare his speech in reply to Hayne; he said, "About thirty years."

Sitting down to his task, the preacher interrogates his text. He asks who wrote it, to whom it was written, for what purpose it was written. He inquires what is the great thought presented in it, and how he can present it to his people. Having discovered and stated the thought, he then begins to recall what he has read and he goes to his memory, or his files, gets out that material and reviews it, finds what is useful to his present purpose, and sets it down. Then he begins to search for new material. All the while his mind is considering the essential values to be presented. Those he sets down as they occur to him. When this assembling process is completed, he begins to set up the framework of his structure. From the thoughts that he has written down, he selects those that are cardinal for his use in unfolding the nature of his subject. He then proceeds to select the matter subsidiary to these different cardinal ideas in the theme, taking what is germane and useful to his purpose, eliminating all the rest.

As he works at this first draft, he meditates upon what he has, considers the people to whom he is to speak, and the adaptability of what he has for them. He ponders its effectiveness in convincing and persuading them, its practical value to them. He returns frequently to the purpose or end he has in view. While he muses the fire burns and his mind glows with the heat of conception, in which the sermon comes to life.

In preparing to preach, the preacher must realize the importance of his complete assimilation of his materials. Whatever he may have in mind of what others have said or done, he must remember, if its re-expression is to be of greatest value, it must be tinged with his own blood. He must have done creative work. When that message is given birth, it must have the mark of his own personality upon it. It is possible for some men to construct sermons made up largely of collections of what other men have said; but such sermons are never vivid or vital. Such preaching does not often prove awakening to those to whom it is delivered. It is what Joseph Parker called "dental preaching"—only from the teeth out. The hard and exhausting work of the preacher takes place when he brings the message to birth.

The accomplishment of this travail of birth of a message is what costs the preacher, but when accomplished, men's hearts rejoice in being present when the message is delivered.

II. *Second, is his physical fitness to preach.*

No one doubts the importance of physical preparation for athletic contests or pugilistic encounters. For weeks and even months, participants are strenuously devoted to their preparation for the expected encounters. The man who lacks either in diligence or continuity in this preparation is never expected to win, however great his knowledge of the technique of the game or the bout. The more formidable the opponent, the more severe must be the discipline. Great artists, musicians, opera stars, actors are not often unaware of the importance of their physical condition for the concerts, or plays, upon the presentation of which their reputation is to be made. Years ago I read one of our greatest actor's unbroken rule, to allow no interruption of his quiet time the last two hours before his public appearance.

But nobody seems to have considered the importance of a like discipline in the preparation of the preacher. Sometimes it seems that the pious make preaching altogether the responsibility of God's Spirit. The greater the preacher's irrelevant activities up to the moment of his entering the pulpit, the greater chance has the Spirit of God to glorify Himself in the use of an exhausted, incompetent instrument! So he carelessly visits or enjoys himself or employs himself without respect to the demands of that crucial hour when he must preach. Most often it is activity in the Sunday school.

He is ambitious to win men and build with them a
men's class. So he organizes and plans and prepares
for that. It meets just before the preaching hour. All
the vitality and strength he possesses is drawn upon
for that. When the preaching hour comes, too often
his fire is spent. He goes with slowed-up tread, and
his speech lacks heat and energy. His eyes may still
be bright, but he lacks the vision to take in what lies
beyond mere sight. Who can imagine any great
preaching by such a man? His force is spent.

I remember the case of such a man. Visiting in a
parish, he was asked at noon to speak at the evening
midweek hour. He accepted, then went off to see the
city. Returning to the manse for tea, it was suggested
he might wish to retire and prepare for his task an
hour before he was due. The New Testament was
placed in his hands, and the subject previously suggested
was called to his mind. But he was too full of talk
and ecclesiastical gossip to allow that precious chance
of an hour more to indulge in it to pass. So he non-
chalantly took the book, glanced at the chapter, and
returned to his consuming interest and conversations.
The hour came for the message. Introduced, he stood
up to speak. Out of an empty mind and exhausted
physique, he addressed a small but exceptionally intelligent group of forty people. An old Scotch elder,
listening for some word of wisdom, was irritated by
the empty utterances poured out. He did not wait for
a private talk, but before the whole group, expounded
the passage with insight and subtle scorn of the preacher
who had come unprepared for the hour. It was embarrassing for the pastor who had presented the preacher

of the evening as his guest. But it was a lesson that young upstart should have taken to heart.

The preacher must, then, prepare himself physically for the preaching hour. He must give attention to the selection of his diet. In his own house, food that is suitable for him should be thoughtfully selected. He should partake of an amount proportioned to his need, but never indulge beyond his power to digest and assimilate. He should jealously observe regular hours for the enjoyment of his meals, whatever may be the custom of the community to which he ministers.

Next to the proper food is proper and regular exercise. This should never be too hard and exhausting. The kind of exercise men of sedentary habit indulge in often does more harm than good. The minister's purpose is not to develop physical prowess, bigness of muscle, the ability to lift great weight or to vault over high hurdles, or to develop abundance of flesh. He should seek the kind and amount of exercise that builds nervous energy, capacity of heart and lungs, vigorous abdominal health, a good throat and healthy vocal chords. He may become a champion in tennis or golf, but championship is not the end to seek. In the choice of exercise, walking is hard to beat, if he learns and observes the proper manner. Practically every vital organ is involved in walking and given its share of exercise. By careful observation, any man can arrive at a knowledge of the distance suited to him. Walking does not make drafts upon the pocketbook, and the speed can be regulated according to his age and strength.

Whatever the form, exercise should be taken regularly and systematically. Most men are liable to delinquency charges in this respect. They did "run well" for a time, like the Galatians, but only for a while. Then they fell by the way. Perhaps they undertook some strenuous activity and suffered in consequence some mishap that is irreparable. But the man who takes regularly a light but general exercise that refreshens his nerves, and keeps supple his muscles, and stimulates his elimination, postpones the day when he enlarges the length of his belt or suffers "the lean and withered shank of age." The amount and kind of exercise suitable for one man would be disaster to another. George Adam Smith was a great walker, stepping it off six miles a day, but his equally notable countryman, Robertson Nicol, found a cold towel-bath and a brisk rough towel rub daily, sufficient for him. The gymnasium, if available and convenient in all seasons, is a good place to patronize, but a walk is available to all men, and there health may be found and kept.

It is a good habit to interrupt one's work, raise the window, take a few deep breaths and slowly exhale, flex the knees, and then by certain movements involve the whole spinal column before sitting down again to the desk. Fresh, pure air thus taken and the aeration of his blood secured, a man can settle down refreshed for a long, hard pull.

Next in importance to regular meals of proper food and regular, suitable exercise in the open air, is sufficient rest. This a man gets in sleep, discontinuance of work, and change of mental activity. The amount of rest a man needs must be determined by several factors. If, by inheritance, he is possessed of a good strong physique and rugged constitution, it may be recovered in a night's sleep. The amount will depend

on the resistance of his natural constitution to the tax
of toil. Some men, like Spurgeon and Napoleon, can
do with four, five, or six hours sleep, but there are
not many who can get sufficient sleep in less than seven
or eight.

By learning to rest five or ten minutes at his desk,
a man may be released from the stress of concentration
and the strain of toil. It may be five minutes' sleep will
be sufficient to release a weary body and brain. It
may be by habits of devotion, when the mind is shifted
from engagement with human personality and earthly
things and the work-worn man talks with God and
gains new power.

> *What change within us, one short hour*
> *Spent in Thy presence will avail to make!*

But sleep is a necessity that nature lays upon all living forms of existence. In some measure, the strongest
and most vital must sleep.

> *The innocent sleep,*
> *Sleep that knits up the ravel'd sleeve of care,*
> *The death of each day's life, sore labor's bath,*
> *Balm of hurt minds, great nature's second course,*
> *Chief nourisher in life's feast.*

Dr. Theodore Ledyar Cuyler, who never lost a day
from illness or other cause for fifty years, called his
sleep on Sunday afternoons his eighth day in the
week. Those Sunday afternoons must have meant much
to him.

One whole day in seven ought to be set aside for
rest. While his people take the first day, we would
advise the preacher to take the last day for his day
of rest. Let it be used in long hours in bed if his sur-

plus reserves are weak. But in whatever way, most men should get away from people, in long walks or hours spent in the city parks, "if he be a city man." Or if privacy is not possible without leaving home, choose some hotel and spend twenty-four hours there occasionally, reading what will refresh and build you up mentally. This cannot be done in hard work, but in what takes your mind out of the creative process. Be amused; follow, if you enjoy it, the plot of some detective story, or revel in some great poetry, or thrill with some great romance. Get away from the task of your other days in the week.

If you are in a rural community, small town, or county seat, God's spaces are not hard to reach. Camera, rod or gun in hand, go out to field, wood, stream, or lake, and put in the day. If these are not your joy, take wife and children with filled lunch baskets and spend the day with them. Too many preachers live for the public and forget that their own are to be known and saved as well as the rest of the world.

We say this weekly rest should be on Saturday for him whose pulpit is his throne. Then, when he faces people who labored for the previous six days, who need refreshment and rest, who are striving to relax, and in a measure to forget the care and responsibility with which they have been taxed, he will come rested and refreshed, with mind alert and vibrancy restored. Because the beginning of such a practice is fraught with difficulty of getting back into the spirit and heart of earnest preparation when he broke it off on Friday, should not deter a man from resting on Saturday. In a short time he will overcome this obstacle and be able on Sunday morning, hours before he has to meet his public, to recover the fire and interest he had on Friday. Flee the suggestion of Saturday midnight toil. It is a dangerous engagement. It is a false way.

Every man, and no one more than the minister, should have an extended leave of absence from his work every year. When that time comes, let him seek some place far from the scenes of his common toil. If he must spend these days or weeks in study and preparation for the year ahead, let him cut his working hours in half. Of all things, let him shun the common practice of supplying vacant pulpits and lecturing to summer conferences. It is not fair to the people who pay him his salary to use his rest time for labor. Some "circumstances alter cases." If such engagements offer him change of scene or contribute to the expansion of his horizon, seaside, mountains, traveling strange countries, then some excuse may be offered for continued toil. But nothing is excusable that does not offer the opportunity to rebuild the wasted strength of previous months of toil.

Again, a man prepares himself for effective pulpit work by cultivating a cheerful and buoyant state of mind. He may, with abounding health, have no difficulty in this. But if he has not been given this buoyancy by natural inheritance, let him remember it can be gained by cultivation and discipline. Cheerfulness can be cultivated by an act of will. The man who determines to put dull care away has made a grand start. If he is introspective by nature, or cursed with an inferiority complex, let him be careful upon what he meditates. Looking within is a bad practice for such men. The prospect is neither pleasing nor profit-

able to them. Do not fail to meditate, but let it be
on prospects with wide and distant horizons and upon
things beyond his own personal possessions.   If you
are prone to melancholy moods, *learn* to *control* them
and to put them from your mind, and fill their place
with subjects of resolution. Seek humorous indulgence.
Find a book, or a companion, or an entertainment that
will compel you to laugh heartily, even uproariously.
Cultivate people that they may come to love you and
you to love them, especially little children and boisterous youth. I am told that Dr. Irving S. Cutter said,
"When concerned about your health consult your
physician. If he says there is nothing seriously wrong
but you still have annoying indispositions, then consult Doctor Quiet, Dr. Diet, and Dr. Merryman." This
is sound advice.

Dr. Lewis O. Brastow, professor of practical theology
in Yale University, says in his *Representative Modern
Preachers* (p. 33): "As preaching is an expression, not
primarily of ideas, opinions, mental judgments, but of
the experiences of the heart, its objects must be to
reproduce, or to develop still further, such experiences
in the souls of the hearers."

Such a reproduction cannot be accomplished by a
tired man. It demands a vibrant soul in a vibrant
frame of flesh and blood. The physical man so conditioned alone is able to stand up to such a task.

CHAPTER XV

THE PREPARATION OF THE PREACHER (II)

The important factor in preaching is the man who
preaches. Consideration must be given to personality
and personality development. The preacher's personality must be related with understanding to the people
to whom he speaks and the time in which he preaches.

Preachers of today live in what is called a scientific
age. That is to say, the atmosphere of the scientist's
laboratory has been carried out over all life engagements, business, industry, and the professions. Where
the social factors are dealt with, one of the marked demands is for social organization. "Organization" is the
word with which men conjure. Great forces and small
must be "organized." "Is he a good organizer?" is
one of the questions most frequently asked about men
recommended for vacant pastorates. "Organizing
ability" is frequently the reason given for the success
of men in high places in the ministry.

Without doubt, this ability is important. Even sermons have to be organized, according to unity, order,
and movement, if they are to be effective. Preachers
must, therefore, develop this gift in some measure.
In handling aggregations of people for effective service,
their organization into smaller groups is essential. But
let no one forget that however great a man's ability,
unless he is able to breathe into these organizations

the breath of life, there can be only the noise of the machine. In such cases little real work will be done unless he can inspire the organization. Some churches have been killed by too many organizations for which there was no adequate inspiration.

Back of the organization must be the man.

When all the factors of success are taken into account, no one factor will be found to bulk bigger in organization than what people call "personality," that "you," that "self," that "man" who makes contacts with people and the public. He gives quality to every word.

> *We listening, learned what makes the might of words—*
> *Manhood to back them, constant as a star.*[1]

What is personality? No definition of personality has been formed so agreeable to all psychologists or even to a great number of them that can be confidently used to end discussion on the subject. Dr. Phillips Brooks said something like this: "Personality is a conscious relationship to God, which through a spirit of obedience to the divine will, unfolds and expands all human powers and brings out the revelation of man." But one cannot forget that some personalities who have been powerful in influencing men have repudiated the consciousness of God. Consciousness of God is the mark of a Christian. It was a marked element in the personality of Brooks and Spurgeon, Beecher and Moody. One needs only a casual acquaintance with Lyman Beecher's family to observe that what distinguished all his children was that, like their father, they were personages—personalities. They were conscious of themselves and of God.

Dr. George A. Coe speaks of personality variously in *What is Christian Education?* but we think he is wise when he says, "To be a person is to have satisfactions and dissatisfactions that are 'one's own' and that are discriminated, compared, and weighed by the one whose 'own' they are, and to act in view of this discrimination, comparison, and weighing."[2] These two definitions differ widely. We might continue with definitions but each of them would differ from all the others as markedly as the personalities of their authors.

In the study of individuals we discover elements recurring with constant regularity that make up what we call personality. Suppose we set down what we observe in those who have been most effective in life's relationships. In so far as our observations have been accurate and discriminating, we shall have material with which we may form concepts of essential personality.

Let me speak of four items thus observed, recurring constantly. First of all, there is self-consciousness, the assurance of one's identity, responsibility, and separateness from all other selves, in contrast to all other peoples and things. In some, this quality is more pronounced than in others. Such persons we describe as egotistic.

In the second place, we have noted power of penetration—the gift of piercing the exterior of things, of going beneath the surface of thought-expression into the heart of concepts stated; sounding the hidden and concealed depth of life. Such persons seem to know what is in man "at first sight."

A third quality is creativeness, the ability to utilize the various elements of environment and content of life for the production of new structures in concepts, conduct, and action. In such persons the constructive imagination functions with more or less effectiveness. Great architects, great administrators, great orators, great novelists, great historians, great preachers, have this element of personality in a marked degree.

There is a fourth quality we call vibrancy—a quality of energy and vigor that lends beauty to ugliness, warmth to coldness, magnetic quality to dullness, attractiveness and inspiration to what, without vibrancy, is dull and heavy. In certain manifestations of public utterance, we call it force. This energy and vigor is self-initiating. We discover the impact which vitality makes, awakening latent qualities in others.

This is a list sufficient to indicate that some analysis of personality has been made, and that much may yet be done, leading to an ultimate and better understanding of oneself and of others, and thus to a great improvement of human relationships. Whatever items we may set down as factors of personality, the important thing is to remember that the improvement of these constituent elements of personality is possible. In proportion as the preacher attends to the development or suppressions of these personality traits, by so much may he greatly increase or retard the impact of his personality upon the people with whom he makes daily contacts.

The occasion in which the preacher makes important contacts with other persons is in preaching. His personality is the most important factor in that contact. To improve his quality, to maintain and increase his vibrancy, to enlarge and strengthen his creative ability, his vitality, the preacher should devote himself diligently. The electric current that carries power in utterance cannot be conveyed through a piece of rubber or a stick of wood.

We wish to recommend three books for reading we consider valuable in the development of personality, with which all preachers ought to be acquainted. The first is *The Improvement of the Mind,* by Isaac Watts, which can be found in most theological libraries or for a reasonable sum may be occasionally obtained from dealers in old, second-hand books. A second is John Foster's *Decision of Character,* an essay to which John R. Mott acknowledges his great indebtedness as one of the most formative influences of his life. The third recommendation is the *Yale Lectures* of Henry Ward Beecher, frequently seen on second-hand bookstore shelves. Probably no more versatile and influential personality ever stood in an American pulpit than Henry Ward Beecher. His adaptability to his audience was unsurpassed, an art that was not only the result of constitutional gifts but of arduous study and constant application to the task of personality development of himself and other men.

Men who cannot possess or read these books recommended may follow definite lines immediately preparatory to their engagement for the next Sunday and directly contribute to the development of their personality to greater magnitude.

1. *Mingle with people and study them in an effort not to spy out the worst self in them but to discover their best self.* This is the value of earnest pastoral care for a congregation. The faithful pastor will prove to himself that there is nothing to compare with sympathetic mingling with people as a "friend of the community at large," in developing personality. In *Jesus*

Came Preaching, Dr. George A. Buttrick has acknowl-
edged his indebtedness to this particular function of
the minister—in building a church, in the discovery
of themes, and in the development of the preacher's
power in uttering his message.[3] In such contacts a
man discovers what gives value to human life. He
discovers also the rocks on which "many a well laden
argosy" has made shipwreck of both faith and life.
In proportion to his diligence and fidelity in such a
ministry, in proportion to the draft made on his own
mind and heart and will for others, so will all the
elements of his own personality be developed. Whosoever will save his life will lose it; but whosoever
will lose his life for Christ's sake in the service of his
fellow-man will find it.

2. *In the second place, let him cultivate the gift
of a confessor.* There are two things a skilled confessor will do. He will become a quiet, interested listener.
By attitude, look, and steady attention he will express
encouragement to the one who has his story to tell,
his confession to make. It is not his place to talk but
to listen; to hear, receive, and keep what is freely
poured into his ear. When the story is told, he may
by a device of question, look, and encouragement to
utter, quicken unreserve in commitment and draw out
the things that might have been forgotten or held back.
Then he will speak his word of instruction, comfort, or
hope. Such a man will feel the expansion of his own
soul and his fellowship with humanity. He will gain
an understanding of the human spirit and increase his
acquaintance with Christ,

> *Who wrought all kind of service with a noble ease*
> *That graced the lowest act in doing it.*

He will succeed in the enlargement of his own personality. He will come to be known as a "preacher who is a good listener," and one who has the pity of God in him for all his fellow-men. Such men pray:

> Immortal love,
> That lives and lives beyond the hour
> When sun, and moon, and countless stars
> Have passed away,
>
> Vouchsafe to me
> Strength, hope, and faith to live right valiantly,
> When knowledge fails and sight grows dim,
> Life's lonely way.
>
> Grant grace to say
> To travelers, worn and broken in life's way,
> Some deathless word of comfort, hope and cheer,
> Throughout each day.
>
> Redeeming love,
> Remembering Thee, specters, black as night
> Slink off and disappear. Eternal morning breaks,
> Day becomes clear!

3. *A man may develop his personality through communion with God.* There is no greater device for the attainment of this inner goal of personality than is this habit of prayer to God, meditation upon His Word, and the maintenance of the mental attitude of listening to what He says when He speaks.

Communion gives elevation to a man's thoughts. It directs the whole of his personality expression to constantly higher levels. It begets an attitude of quietness and poised expectancy of definite indications in his own life's directions. For God does answer him. Something like this happened in Paul's life when he heard the call from Macedonia. Assuredly gathering that it was of the Lord, he followed the call and carried the gospel to eastern Europe.

It is also the way to develop the mediator quality in a preacher's personality. Surely this is one of the greatest virtues a people ever discover in their minister. They see in him God's representative with them. He is God's ambassador. He is God's agent and mouthpiece, through whom God speaks to them. Everybody may not have said so, but deep in their hearts, they know it is only to such men He commits His mind. Men who have not held communion with Him, those who are strangers to Him, who have not His counsel and love, who are not *en rapport* with Him, cannot communicate God to anyone.

> *In the mind upright and holy*
> *In the heart contrite and lowly*
> *God reveals Himself,*
> *The secret of the world.*

If he be a preacher who has such a heart and mind, he will be a mediator of God to men.

And he will gain their confidence that he can mediate for them with God. The files of the telegraph offices of the world will offer abundant evidence that this conviction has gripped men's minds. Loved ones fall sick and their condition grows desperate; then men and women's hearts turn to some beloved minister now far away and they send a wire, "John in the hospital.

Condition desperate. Pray for us." Now, why do they do that? Because that minister is a mediator for them and because they believe the prayer of a righteous man availeth much in its working. He knows the way to God's dwelling. He has been there often for them. He is human in spirit. He knows the paths that men tread. He knows their needs and he knows how to tell God all about them and that need. He is a mediator. His personality has developed in two dimensions —manward and Godward. In him God dwells and humanity lives. When such a man preaches and prays, men feel God is nigh.

Such a man is given to prayer for his people. They are "on his mind." He thinks about them—about their joys, their cares, their victories, their defeats, their burdens, their bondages, their temptations, their sicknesses, their sins, their hopes, their fears. He makes provision in the regular schedule of his engagement for some time to pray for his people, when he carries them up to God with all these things that fill their lives. Intercession for those to whom he ministers becomes part and parcel of this preacher's daily schedule of work. Such a man's heart is constantly enlarged with the cause of God and men. When it is so, the whole circumference of his personality is enlarged. His mind becomes enriched with life and the history of God with humanity. And when he preaches, there is the evidence of it in the opulence of his mind, the tenderness of his heart, the sweep of his vision, the evidence of his struggle for worthy and great causes. It is indisputable because all this gets into his message, not in the form which it has come to him, but in that recreated output his ever-enlarging personality expresses.

4. *Let the preacher make every Sabbath service an act of consecration, of commitment of himself to God to be used by Him.* After all, in a world morally astray and spiritually deficient, the preacher is not sufficient uttering his own opinions and intellectualisms. For centuries, wise men have spoken. But no sadder spectacle confronts us than the futility of wisdom. "When in the wisdom of the world, the world by wisdom knew not God, it pleased God by the foolishness of preaching to save them that believe." The preacher then must utter the wisdom of God. If he is to do so, he must give God a chance to speak through him. He must, therefore, by an act of commitment of himself to God's control, be fitted for such use. Certainly such a commitment, in itself, is an ascent to larger concepts, larger power, wider horizons, and more effectual utterances. No man will deny this who believes that God is. By so much, then, it must be evident that his personality is expanded by every such commitment. He comes to his task with a consciousness of resources learning alone cannot give, which scholarship cannot give, which contacts, influential and effective among men, cannot guarantee. He comes with an assurance that cannot be dashed by the skilled, the learned, and the influential. He is not afraid of the faces of men. He knows God is at his back, giving him the message, providing the power of conviction necessary to accomplish the divine purpose.

"Here is the difference," says John Oman, "between speaking from what God has said and done in the past; the latter, even if from the revealed, is from it as the revealing, is valid for us now as it ever was in the past. The only true authority is God's truth itself and its own witness to itself; and you speak with its authority only when you speak that which you know and testify that which you have seen."[4] Just so. By this faithful act of commitment of himself to God, to be used of Him, God gets the chance to speak to him and through him. A man who is the channel of God's utterance is a far bigger man thereby than he could possibly be without God.

5. *For the enlargement of one's personality, and the gain of greater effectiveness in preaching, a man should cultivate the habit of trusting his own mind to do its work when the hour is come.*

"Trust thyself," said Emerson. All things else respond to this. The failure to be courageous enough to do this has put many men in hobble-straps all their life. If it is not learned in youth and young manhood, it is difficult to venture that way when the years have passed. For it demands courage, the courage of real adventure into unknown and uncertain fields of human experience. Two men after a preaching service walked down a city street. One had just preached without a scratch of a pen before him. They walked in silence for a block. Then suddenly the listener turned to the preacher and said, "Do you always speak without your paper?"

"Usually," said the preacher.

"How do you do it?"

"You have to begin early: dare to fail, if it comes to that; then trust your own mind and speak as God gives you utterance."

That is enough to say, commit yourself to God, trust your own mind, and speak as God gives you utterance. It is an adventure that develops faith in oneself, faith in God's faithfulness. Such a process develops personality qualities of tremendous value and power of impact upon the minds of men.

Such are some of the elements in the process of spiritual culture and preparation of men to preach. This spiritual culture is the kind of culture the pulpit needs in every land; but nowhere is it a "consummation devoutly to be wished" more than in America. This, yet a new land and young nation, has so many conflicting cultures engaging the attention of our people that spiritual culture has been restricted and even shut out of our lives. It is interesting to note the number of book clubs, reading clubs, professional clubs, social clubs, organized in every community or for which propaganda through the press, the radio, and the mail is carried on, seeking the patronage of our people, and, at the same time, to observe how little of it is specifically organized for the enrichment of the preacher's acquaintance with God. It was a wise observer of human affairs who told three hundred ministers gathered for a summer conference that, if they wanted to do something worth while and different in their parishes, let them go home and organize Bible-reading clubs for their people. Excellent suggestion. If this is too hard a task, they can at least have one for themselves. A man may develop his personality by determining upon the spiritual culture of his own spirit, whatever else he may not know. By doing so, all other cultures will find their proper claim on his personality, and passing through such a medium will make their proper contribution for enrichment of the preacher and the utterance he makes. An opulent mind in a vibrant personality is the need of today, greater than any other that may be mentioned. Preparation of the schools is only preparatory. Life is the great matter. Life, rich in the knowledge of God and men, is the only material from which great preaching can come. Men of such "weight" are, alone, big enough to preach with the power that moves the world to better things. Personality, its enrichment and development, that is what the preacher should seek for himself. Then, whatever he touches, or whatever passes through him, will be illuminated, vitalized, and made enlisting.

CHAPTER XVI

THE INSPIRATION OF THE PREACHER

THERE cannot be much useful preaching without inspiration to preach. The sermon plan, the chosen text, the illustrative material, the method of treatment, the order of arrangement, the quality of the style—all are important; but unless the heat and glow and passion of inspiration are present, the sermon will fail in the borning. All hangs on the inspiration that vitalizes and moves the preacher. "Preaching in the broadest sense is simply the impact which one personality makes on those within his sphere of influence."[1] But "impact" implies a movement that has been initiated by something or someone outside of and back of, that is, a power, a force, a weight. A man feels that which is bearing him up and forward; something that helps him to see a vision before him; something that gives utterance to him; that awakens memories; recalls past experience; gives insight, quickening expression, and that fuses all in new meanings and concepts that seem to utter themselves. Inspiration, subtle, indefinable as it is, is that something which electrifies and thrills the preacher and enables him to communicate in kind to his audience. Under inspiration, his word and message leap out to touch his hearers with magnetizing contact. They are thrilled and moved hearing him. At such a time the personality of the preacher is aflame.

The problem is, how may the preacher seize and hold this divine *afflatus*? In the quiet of his study, when preparing for the occasion to which he is now come, he felt the warmth and glow of composition; but too often, when the hour came to speak, he felt the chilling cold of fireless hearts. All wires to the power-house were down. Connections between him and the receiver were broken. Pictures and dreams of other hours had faded away and would not return. To use a word of the old Spiritualists, the spirit would not "materialize" before the faces of men.

Can such a situation of inspiration, which makes the message live and run with power into the mind and hearts of men, be made more certain and constant? If so, how? We offer some suggestions:

1. *Inspiration, at a given hour, will depend on the experimental history of the man.* If, to use the word of Sylvester Horne, "the one supreme qualification for the ministry is a soul aflame," we must remember flames do not start suddenly except in highly combustible material. The fiercest are often slowly awakened. There must be some live coals upon which a breeze may blow before the flame that spreads and enkindles others may be developed.

a) *The preacher must have made some contacts with God.* He must have gained by actual touch with reality, and participation in results of testing, a consciousness of the quickening of mind and heart and will, before he can recall such experience in the hour of uttering his message. He cannot establish inspiration offhand nor by the *ipse dixit* of his speech communicate it to others. To get aflame he must, beforehand, accumulate materials that burn.

Hence, those great events of the soul related to God must have preceded the hour of his preaching. He must, even as Nicodemus, be able to say, "We know—because," or like Paul, "I know Him—and am persuaded"; or like Peter and other disciples, "We cannot but speak things we have both seen and heard." When a man has had such an experience it becomes a fire in his bones, and, though the flame fall low, it may be raised again.

b) *Such a man becomes diligent in the observation and accumulation of the data of the gospel history,* especially of people who have been born again and who have a supporting history. In the hour when his own heart grows cold and his eye of faith is dimmed, or when icebergs appear chilling the waters of life, then a remembrance of what God *has* wrought in *other* men will stir up the faith that has died down in him. He comes to talk about the possibilities of a man and the hope of his recovery at his worst; but somehow or other, only the hopelessness of failure is before him. Then he remembers that a man on his way to hale believers to prison and persecution was suddenly arrested and changed. He was a chosen vessel unto God to stand before kings and to declare what God can do for a man and what a salvation Jesus Christ has brought. Remembering, the preacher can see what God has *done*. He thinks of what a change of front was made, what motivation to sacrifice and service was applied, what transference of estimates was effected, what a gift for interpretation was bestowed, what boldness and power were granted for high effort and noble living. Lingering over such facts, finding them repeated over and over in the lives of men, he feels the certainty of their possible repetition in the lives of men before him, and his heart is warmed with the vision.

There are men who have picked up their Augustine and read again what God did to deliver a man from the bondage of his lusts. Remembering the satisfaction the soul finds in God, just before they went to speak, they felt a fresh glow of the power on which they must depend. One I have known has had his confidence in the fact of conversion as a possible experience for men at their worst reënkindled by those lives in Masefield's *Everlasting Mercy*, where Saul Kane describes the amazing glory of the lighted mind. If you know such men, whose experience supports and confirms your own, the recollection of such will rekindle the fire again in your heart. While a man muses upon such accumulated experience, the *fire burns*.

2. *Inspiration will depend on the preacher's contact with and response to human need.* Stirring as contact with physical distress and material need are to the man of sympathy, it is not of these alone I am thinking. The curse of poverty, and the crush of sweatshops, and the cold of empty hearthstones, the squalor of tenements, the pain of cancerous economic injustice, have power to stir a man to speak out boldly in God's name on behalf of those who suffer. But there are too many men who never make contact with these distresses except by proxy. Proxitic contacts do not burn men's souls like direct touch. It takes imagination, keen and constructive, to profit from contacts by proxy. It too

often lacks the actual element of experience to fire a man's soul.

Most people, though not always capable of defining their need, have in some measure felt their need of God. Without God, life is a short and terrible tragedy, a brutal thing, mean and groveling. Without God, a man's life is subject to masterful and enslaving instincts, appetites, and desires that continually get behind the wheel and drive without sense or reason, toward death. Yet there is conscience in the front seat with a man's soul. Conscience torments, cramps, and condemns him for his folly. But he will not listen to conscience and take its advice. He has not considered "the spirit of man is the lamp of Jehovah searching all his innermost parts."[2] Fear, timidity, and cowardice take possession of the man. Such a man needs to have some seer who can see that he needs God and who is able to lead him to God.

Now, not all preachers are sensitive to such needs nor intelligent in the way of such leadership. Twenty years ago two men in a great Midwestern city were pastors of two congregations. One Sabbath afternoon, one of these men spoke in the other's church on "Saving a Soul alive." The next day he had a message from his friend asking for an interview. They had it while driving about the city. In this drive, the man seeking the conference said, "I was greatly interested in what you said yesterday in my church. Since you spoke, I have been facing this fact, if any man wanting to find God should come to my study wanting to find the way to Jesus Christ I would not know what to do with him. Can you tell me how to lead a man to Christ?"

Here was a man of considerable preaching gift who did not know how to meet the principal responsibility a preacher has to meet. Such a man could not, therefore, have inspiration for his work from his knowledge of a soul's need. The thirty-second Psalm would be "Greek" to him. He should read the Penitential Psalms and those great passages of God's Word where the longing souls yearn for God. He should search his own greatest need to its depths. Then let him ask what is God's attitude toward one like himself. He will discover God is eager to help such as he. Out of such a discovery he will be able to lead other searching souls home to God. Eager, seeking men and women sit before the preacher in every congregation that assembles. The remembrance of the fact ought to stir him with glowing power to plead with men to turn with full surrender to God.

Then there are lonely souls that need companionship. They are found everywhere. Men and women, young and old, for whom the longing for companionship, for the privilege of sharing life, for love, is eating at their vitals; for whom no cure has been found. It is possible that in country and in town, in every urban center, more people can be found whose life is a burning desert for want of companionship and love than for any other need. If you read such a book as *The Gold-coast and the Slums*,[3] or *God in the Slums*,[4] it is difficult to escape the suggestion that such loneliness and the fear of its continuance accounts for their making a wreck of life. It was in such hours they started on the way of shame and degradation that became their destiny. "She weeps sore in the night, and her tears are on her cheeks; among all her lovers she has none to comfort her. All her friends have dealt treacherously with her and they have become her enemies." "Is it nothing to you, all ye that pass by?"[5] Can a preacher think of such need for companionship and not feel a quickening of his own heart to speak words of comfort and direction?

Man needs comfort, assurance, and hope as he faces the inexplicable mysteries, the terrible inequalities and contradictions life presents. Over against this terrifying fact of life we have a gospel that does not deny it, or run away from it, or try to belittle it. It meets it valiantly. Whatever a purely exemplary gospel of life may claim in exalting the virtue of courage and fortitude in living, so also may the preacher of the gospel of Jesus claim. But living bravely, going down in defeat with an unbroken spirit, being valiant for the sake of being valiant, is not all. Though with Henley, a man midst the "fell clutch of circumstance," who has not "winced nor cried aloud," may be striving to be brave, simply in loyalty to the mastership of his own soul, he has not gained all the man in Christ has to gain. He has, also, the belief and the assurance that there is something in this conflict that is better than even recognizing the bitterness of the conflict or the perfection of self-mastery.

Such a man may have the consciousness of being leagued with God Himself in the redemption of a world through suffering. He is not called to live bravely and die valiantly simply for the sake of bravery and valiancy. He is fighting in the consciousness of life that is for two worlds, not for one. He is living valiantly, now knowing he will come ultimately to a perfect realization of fellowship with God Himself. The true preacher has the inspiration of a problem of suffering and mystery and utter defeat from the world viewpoint, that finds solution in an incomparable victory.

Let him remember the suffering and cross of Jesus. His enemies heaped upon Him not only suffering but shame also when they hung Him upon a tree. So far as moral worth and excellence are considered, He was incomparable. Yet they oppressed, afflicted, and killed Him. But after two days and nights were passed in the darkness of death, the morning came, light broke through. That sunrise shed its glory on the darkness to which humanity is subject. It is the privilege of every preacher to live through that agony and utter his message in that glory. If he does so, then the inspiration that lifts a man to noble heights will come to him when he faces his people.

When a man preaches, he must remember the deadliness of sin. It is no afternoon tea affair atmosphere into which the gospel of Jesus Christ must be brought. It is a plague atmosphere that has swept over the earth and settled its destruction on the race. There is a conflict of war. This conflict is not simply a skirmish of troops playing at war in a summer camp, with innocuous bombs and fake maneuvers. The preacher must realize, and it must become the permanent consciousness of his mind, as with the Apostle Paul, we *war*, not against flesh and blood, but we war against principalities and powers. These foes in this conflict are not merely threatening war. They are at war. They will not be satisfied except in the total possession of the land and citizens for which they fight. The bitterness, the brutality, the effrontery, the uncompromising violence of Japan in China or Hitler toward central Europe are nothing compared with the war that sin makes in its assault on the sons of men and God. The misfortune that has so often befallen the race is that preachers without imagination to construct the situation or see the issues of this war with sin have stood up to preach. To them it has been simply a debate, a clash of opinions, or at most a conflict that may be won with the mild moralities of education. Such preaching is too often from the lips out. It does not rise from the deep recesses of a heart broken by the sorrow that sin has wrought.

A young preacher not long since, talking about the world conflict that nations are waging now, said to me, "For three weeks the terribleness of this world situation has rested on my heart as a great burden and tomorrow I must speak." I went to hear him, and I could easily believe that he had the evening before spoken the truth. That Sunday morning he spoke like one inspired. It was a trumpet note he sounded to war-worn troops. In this young man this conviction had taken possession of a prophet of God that war is on. It determined his speech when the hour for speaking came.

3. *The inspiration of the preacher will also depend upon his concept of the value of his vocation to the world.*

Has there ever been a time to send men into the ministry who are uncertain about preaching being the most effective instrument of God for saving the world? If I were set to examine a young man as to his motives for entering the gospel ministry, I would want to know how he looks on this task. What are the issues it represents? Are these merely professional? Are they debatable? Are they temporal and expedient? Does preaching deal with the eternal, with matters that determine the destinies of men? Has preaching dealt with the vital issues of the world from the days of the Old Testament prophets down to this very hour?

The concept a man has of his task is most important in determining the atmosphere that will surround him, the spirit that will be in him when he preaches. I have seen young men in the pulpit who, if they had the spirit of the occasion and opportunity when they preached that they had when they contested for an oratorical prize or fellowship, would have taken much more seriously their opportunity.

Again I am thinking of a man who was a master when he arose in his literary club to debate or sketch a policy of social reform or review the philosophy of some "latest book," but when he rose to preach, he was as uninspiring as a goldfish swimming around its crystal bowl. He was not moved by the spirit of a messenger, a witness, an advocate, or a prophet then. The effect upon his audience was soporific to some and tiresome to others. If he knew anything about the history of his vocation, the burning of the idols under Paul, or the burning of vanities by Savonarola, of the men and women moved to great deeds, there was no indication of it in that hour when he preached.

Let the preacher acquaint himself with what preaching has done through the centuries, if he lacks convic-

tion as to the dignity and power of his vocation. Let
him follow the example of Sylvester Horne, who advised
all preachers whose hearts are cold to acquaint
themselves with Athanasius.[6] Let him study the life of
Savonarola, when his great awakening had come; of
John Knox, who ruled Scotland in his time and left an
atmosphere that is vital with the tradition of his preaching to this hour; of John Wesley and George Whitefield, of Charles H. Spurgeon and Dwight L. Moody,
if he thinks men of the pulpit are not men of power.
By such acquaintance, every time he stands up to preach
he may feel the grandeur of his opportunity and the
measure of his responsibility before God and men.

4. There are lesser values than these, of which we
must take account, which affect a preacher's inspiration when he stands up to preach. *Inspiration often is
cooled or warmed by the attitude of the audience to
which he speaks.* Some men are inspired by their knowledge of a spirit of opposition confronting them. So
was Henry Ward Beecher preaching in England during
the Civil War. The knowledge that he would be heckled
or be the focus for violent demonstration was like the
smoke of battle to an old war horse; it gave him spirit
and power. Others are silenced by such a situation.
They can only speak with men who are kindly disposed
to the message they bring. In either case a man must
learn to adjust himself, and in some measure, strive to
create the atmosphere in which he can flourish best. In
any event, before the end he must leave the definite
message which has been committed to him to bring.

Again, some men are susceptible to the size of the
audience they have to meet. There are those who speak
best to the small group. They feel easiest when they

do not have too many cups to fill. Others fail unless they have the crowds. One of the most capable men that ever preached was Charles H. Spurgeon. He seemed so inspired by the content of his message, the crowd, whether small or great, profited by the mighty truth he preached to all alike. If a man needs the larger group to attain his best, then he must take into account many factors in building up his audience. For example, such a man will see to it that they are seated neither too far away from the preacher nor from each other. The electric current inspiration carries and by which men and women are drawn cannot leap over wide spaces from preacher to hearer or from hearer to hearer. They must be within the radius of the electric spark.

The inspiration of another man depends on the intelligence of the audience to which he speaks, their economic and social state, or their intellectual and spiritual interest. If he speaks to an audience aware of what is going on in the world, then he feels the power of a message that appeals to such interests and that is sustained and held by the message he has prepared in a like environment.

There are multitudes of men who could preach acceptably to a company of people from the suburbs, but who would have no word to a city mission in the slums.

The inspiration that comes to men from these lesser conditions is only secondary and of little importance in the end. Every man must remember the best fountains of life spring from the experience of a man in communion with God and from brooding over a sinful world that must be redeemed. And that is accomplished not by the power of human effort, or devices, but by God's Spirit, saith the Lord of hosts.

Chapter XVII

THE PREPARATION OF THE PEOPLE

The preacher must accept some responsibility for the conditioning experience of his people when they come to hear him preach.

I. *This will depend, first, on their persuasion as to his attitude toward them.* Some years ago a young man, after his first year in the seminary, decided to discontinue his preparation to be a minister on the ground that he was not interested in people. If he was correct in his self-analysis, he was undoubtedly correct in his decision to turn to some other vocation. He had solid reasons for making the decision to change his course. Was it Phillips Brooks or John Oman who said that the man who is not interested in people is never called to preach? He does not have the Love that undertook to save the world. That was the motive back of Jesus Christ's ministry. That also was the motive of Paul's work—"that by all means he might save some."

The preacher who continues in a given place for a number of years, vibrant, alert, and loving people, gains one great advantage—he gets to know the people and they to know him. When he preaches they are prepared in a large measure to hear what he has to say, unless he is like the Scottish minister in the story.

"What sort o' a minister have ye, Donald?"

"Dod, man, he's no muckle. Sax days of the week

he's invisible, and on the seventh, he's incomprehensible!"

No element in the personality of Henry Ward Beecher so prepared him to preach as did his *deep interest in people,* not only the individual, but the mass of people. Humanity was his passion. He believed in their possibilities. He knew their difficulties, their perplexities, their despairs, their ambitions, their hopes; and he sympathized with them. This passion for the people he developed by contact with all sorts of people. He boasted that there was not a single pilot on the ferry-boats between Brooklyn and New York he did not know. He made it his business to know them, to inquire of them and to learn of them. When he built his church in Brooklyn, he required architects and builders to remember the people, and to incorporate in their plans what *the people* would require to feel at home in the building. So also in his sermons. Each sermon was prepared with the individual and the audience before him. The inquiry in the back of his mind was, "How will this strike them?" "The people" was the fundamental ground of his argument in his great lecture, *The Reign of the Common People,* delivered in Great Britain. In that address, he contrasted the systems of government in the Old Country with the fundamental political concepts of the New. In the former there were three groups: first, the king; second, the nobleman and the gentry; third, the great mass of mechanics, farmers, men following the water, and all laboring persons. The first two dominated their political scientists and legislators. In America the first two classes did not exist. Here only, that great mass of common folk were found. For them government was instituted. The guarantee of their rights, their interest, their possessions, was the consideration first, last, and all the time in the purpose of their statesmen. This was, therefore, the fundamental element in the American theory of democratic government. The priority of the people was also fundamental in Henry Ward Beecher's theory of the church and of preaching. The result was "the common people heard him gladly."

No man can read the New Testament without a consciousness of Jesus' conviction of their importance; and of His love for them, of His living, serving, and dying for them, all of them, the well-to-do and the poor, the high and the low, the law abiding and the criminals. So "the common people heard Him gladly." Turning the pages of the New Testament, from Nazareth to Calvary you hear the tramp of their feet as they follow Him and listen to the gracious words that fall from His mouth.

Again I say, the great advantage of a continuous pastorate for the vibrant minister lies in the fact that people learn of his interest in human beings. He knows their circumstance, their mode of living. Their plans and purposes gain his enlistment; their despairs confront him and envelop him; their problems are *his* problems. They know he cannot prepare his message and leave them out. Therefore, they are ready to hear what he will say to them out of his love for them.

II. *A man prepares his audience by preaching to the "bosom and business of men."* When this record is made for a while it gets noised abroad. The people note the preacher's conduct, they observe his sympathies, mark his conversation, and as the weeks slip away, they record his successive sermon subjects. They learn what dominates his mind. If he has a true shepherd's interest in the souls of his people, they know he cares for them and that he talks about what he cares for.

In his *The Work of Preaching*, Arthur S. Hoyt said, "The sermon has sometimes lost its grip upon men by its aloofness of thought, its ignorance of what was really going on in the hearts of men, and its unreality of style, not using the best speech of daily contacts. It would be far better for the preacher to study such matters of the plain people and of common speech used by John Bright and Abraham Lincoln."[1] Such men spoke to the bosom and business of men.

But, best of all, the sermon is the opportunity of the man who knows his Bible; for the Bible speaks to the business and bosom of men. From Genesis to Revelation it uses the best language of the people. The Bible deals with their daily engagements, their practical contacts with each other in the market-place and the home, whatever version is consulted. It talks of men who tilled the soil, who had flocks of sheep and droves of cattle, who accumulated wealth, bought properties, and sold them. The reader comes upon leaders of men and learns of the motives that moved them, by which they ruled. He comes upon jealousies, covetousness, and acquisitiveness, hatred, and greed in many bosoms. He learns of men who went down to the seas in ships and did business in great waters, men who discovered hidden treasures and sold all they had to buy the field where they were; men who plowed and sowed and reaped, men who were profligate and men who hoarded, men who fished all night and caught nothing, men who took high office and prostituted it to violence and unworthy gain. All these and other interests and activities of mind and heart, the reader of the Bible comes upon. The preacher who has any interest in people cannot help but find the secrets of the hearts and the problems of the minds he daily contacts in his own town or in his own Bible. Amid these like interests and surroundings, the preacher's people live. There, religion is put to the test and proved. A religion that has nothing to do with the business and bosoms of people is of no value. Sermons are primarily religious utterances, and they must speak of religion in daily relationships. In such relationships men lose their souls; and there also they must find their salvation and prove the reality of its vision and its discipline.

This does not mean that such a preacher will always speak popular and pleasing words. I listened one morning to a young preacher who had not sufficient courage to deal with the frivolities of his people. First, he denied any knowledge of theology or intention to speak as a theologian. He prefaced his mentioning their indulgences with a confession of his own, but not with any note of repentance or word of condemnation. My host was a man a few years younger than the preacher. When we returned to his home, his first question was, "Well, what did you think of the sermon?" I replied, "It is far more important to know what you thought of it." The note of irritation with which he had questioned me made me expect a prompt reply. It came, "I think a man who apologizes for his timid utterance in rebuking sins and who belittles the science (Theology) he represents is not qualified to preach." This young man expected his preacher to be as earnest and courageous as his doctor ought to be with people who

are sick. The preacher was not aware of revealing his
own incompetency as viewed by one of his hearers, to
whom frivolity in religion was a grievous sin and the
curse of his people. Sin is something that needs to be
dealt with courageously by one who is facing it, and
with disciplinary earnestness. The reaction from timid,
apologetic dealing with sin made clear what one
thoughtful young man, a university graduate, thought
of that kind of preaching. He seldom went to hear
the preacher nearest to his home.

III. *Again, people are prepared to hear a man they
discover is not parochial in his interests but world-
minded in his outlook.* I doubt if there ever was a time
when this would not have been a determining factor in
the preparation of an audience to hear what their
preacher had to say. If so, that time has gone by. In
a day when the daily press spreads the news of the
world before its readers at the breakfast hour it is not
a time for the parochial-minded to expect to be heard.
When the telephone was invented and developed into
practical use, the sphere of Community, State, and
National interest was enlarged. When the radio, with
its marvelous expansion of audition, was brought to
millions of homes in every nook and corner of the
world, parochial-minded people were banished from
all centers of human influence and life. While, on the
one hand, the physical world had been shrunk to
neighborhood proportions, on the other, human interest
and human responsibility had expanded to take in the
world. We are no longer subject to national interest
and engagements alone. We are now literally dominated by the alarms and proposals of all nations of
the earth. When the American market collapses, prices

for the necessities of life are affected in India and China and even to the farthest margins of the world. Women in America bob their hair, and Korean women who made hair-nets for the American market are impoverished. Some virulent disease attacks the people in Turkey and the near East, and in two or three short years it decimates the population of the Occident. Wild-eyed, desperate men in the Ghetto of New York project their political and social theories on the people of Russia, and in a few short years their Bolshevism rolls back on the United States like a wave of the sea that threatens to inundate the country. The President of the United States displaces the gold standard of the financial world with a silver standard, and the next morning Downing Street in London and the Bourse in Paris and Berlin are in a frenzy. These are not isolated incidents pointing to remote connections in political, national, racial, financial, and human life. They are commonplaces of a world that is solidly knitted into an organic whole. "No man liveth unto himself," it makes no difference who he is or where he is. He is now a citizen of the world. The primary question is, how vitally does he live in it? If he does not live vitally there is no body of thinking men and women who care to hear him when he speaks.

When he does live constantly in eager identification with his fellow-citizens of the world, then people find it out. They know when he speaks it will be from the world environment in which he lives. He will expand their horizon. He will enable them to live more abundantly. Such a man has his mind on humanity when he prepares to preach. They will listen when he speaks.

This world contact of religious and moral ideas and

movements will be particularly important. The people
may not have clearly defined their convictions but they
still expect their minister to be the moral and religious
authority in their midst. There is no sphere of human
interest that has expanded its horizon, multiplied its
activities, or developed its consciousness of solidarity
and accepted larger responsibilities more than has the
religious world. Seventy years ago the great religious
organizations had little to do with each other. The "sin
of occasional hearing" was punished with ecclesiastical discipline. The concepts of religious experience
were standardized and measured by loyalties to creeds.
Religious faith that faces mountains to remove in social, industrial, economic, and business relationship
was not required to be implemented in social organization for such purposes then. Very religious and
spiritually-minded people lived remotely so far as the
curses and corruptions of sin in all human society
were concerned. That sort of religious living was entirely satisfactory both to saints and sinners. Now we
are confronted with a demand that religion be practically effective in changing the world and in removing
these obstacles to wholesome, just, and healthful daily
living. Religion must be useful. The instances in which
it has proved its practical efficiency are multiplied, and
these besiege the moral and religious leaders for consideration. There lies before me as I write the monthly
magazine of a great industrial corporation containing
the speech of its president in which is indicated the
change in current business concepts in human relations.
His subject is "Good Will." He says:

"The wages paid to the worker has created more
problems and resulted in more ill will than almost any

other single factor. We can no longer think of business as existing solely for profit. It exists in part to provide men with the means of earning livelihoods and even ahead of profit must come fair wages." He refers to past concepts. "How blind we were in those days! We thought if we paid a going wage, the wage paid in other industries, we were doing all that was fair and necessary. But we weren't. The going wage was too low. Men with families couldn't live decently on it. We didn't mean to be hard in those days. We just couldn't see as we can see now that permanence and success can be built only when we pay fair wages to our workers and when we have their good will."[2]

Such expressions of lofty idealism in human relationship are a challenge to the contemporary religious leaders of such men. It demands a deeper sounding of the depths of the gospel of Jesus, from which that president took the subject of his address, and a more penetrating study of the implications of that gospel in all human relations. Provincial-minded preachers will never be listened to when preaching to such an age as ours, and the man who has caught the mind of the New Testament will not be satisfied with a surface acquaintance with such a gospel. The people will come to know to what heights and depths and lengths and breadths the preacher has explored and tested in human relations. If he has made great adventures in seeking to know and to apply this good news, he cannot keep it out of his preaching. The people will want to hear him. And what is far better and inevitable, they will follow him.

IV. *People are prepared for the regular hearing of the preacher whose message grows out of his pastoral contacts with his people.* A year and a half since a min-

ister desiring a change of pastorate called on me and
asked for my commendation to a certain well endowed
down-town church in a great city. He revealed to me
that his principal desire for that particular pulpit was
its primary requirement for preaching and its secondary
requirement of pastoral visiting. Pastoral visitation he
loathed. How much effective preaching can a man do
who does not have the shepherding spirit? I would
be doubtful of his high achievement as a preacher.
Preaching is vital only when those fundamental sympathies and sensibilities involved in and calling for
contacts with people are urgent and compelling. A man
who has no touch with men and women who face temptations, the conflict of opposing interests, the disasters
of life's calamities, and the shame of its calumnies—
how can such a man be an efficient preacher? If it were
possible to measure a man's capacities for friendship,
for sharing life experiences of joy and sorrow, of victory and defeat, his willingness and ability to bear
other people's burdens and so fulfill the law of Christ,
we should discover one of the first qualities for great
preaching, at least for acceptable preaching.

There comes to mind a man whom I have never heard
preach but whom I have known for many years. I have
never heard any praise of his preaching. All that has
ever been said is in praise of his shepherding. Nevertheless there is not a Sunday when he does not preach
to "good" audiences. The people come regularly and
in large numbers to hear what their "beloved Doctor"
has to say to them. Many young men have followed
his example and "gone into the ministry." When one
inquires into this man's preaching, he finds that every

Sunday's sermon reflects the parish life of the past week
in some measure; now little, and again much.

Who could number the secrets such a man carries
in his bosom, the joys that have been shared with him
in public and private, the rosy ambitions of youth, the
serious proposals of maturity, the struggles for existence, the temptations of leisure, the staggering defeats and the hard won victories in the combat of life,
the hopes and fears of his people that pull at his heart-
strings all the day long! When such a man reads his
Bible, he does not often have to search for a text. They
have called to him at every corner of the street in his
pastoral rounds, and he goes back to his Book to read
them over again as echoed in the highways and byways
of his daily contacts.

V. *A preacher prepares a people if they get the conviction that he has some word from God to give them
on which they can depend.* A modern critic of religion
says, "Many reasons have been given why people do
not go to church as much as they once did. Surely the
most important reason is that they are not so certain
that they are going to meet God when they go to church.
If they had that certainty they would go."[3] It is possible there is some important sense in which this most
"important reason" is true. But nobody in my acquaintance wants to meet God except as revealed in Jesus
Christ. I certainly do not. I know of no concept of
God apart from Jesus Christ which the modern Gentile
mind conceives to be worthy; worthy the consideration
of thoughtful people as well as those who are not
thoughtful, that does not conceive of Him as a righteous
God possessed of that penetration that sees through all
camouflages, that in the simple language of the Hebrews

is as "a consuming fire." I can't help but feel Mr.
Lippman has allowed himself to fall into the concepts of God found in the New Testament, which reveals
a God of love. But Mr. Lippman does not believe the
New Testament speaks with *authority to this age*. His
words do not bear out my experience. That experience
is—men who do not believe in Jesus Christ and the
revelation of God He has brought do not want to
meet God.

Mr. Lippman talks about this modern age that is
too intelligent to believe the Bible. He may be able
to speak for them, but he should remember that the
age that does not know Jesus Christ has not the knowledge that fits them to meet God. Those who have accepted the gospel know God as their Father and they
have an Advocate with the Father. Without Him we
do not want to meet God, but with Him we have no fear.
His perfect love shed abroad in our hearts casts out
fear. Acceptance of the Christ whom the New Testament presents makes people want to go to church. Men
go to church because the church has a message, which
accepted, prepares them to meet God—not as a consuming fire, but as a loving heavenly Father.

The missing note in Mr. Lippman's writing is of the
experience and power of the love of Christ. This is the
truth that makes men free, that makes them seek the
worship of the church. When a preacher witnesses to
this love, people go to church to hear it. But those do
not go who are obsessed with the pleasures of the world,
who are beguiled by the deceitfulness of riches, who feel
intellectually superior to the acceptance of his message,
who are beguiled by the vain philosophies that offer no
certain word about time, eternity, sins forgiven, and

hope of life beyond the tomb. The church, that institution founded on Jesus Christ, constituted by those
who believe the revelation He has brought, if it has
lost its power, should scrutinize its experience, its message, and its life. The church should ask: Do we accept the message and live the life that proves our belief
in Him and the word He has brought? Preachers who
stand up to proclaim their intellectualism, or the opinions of men concerning social redemption without Christ,
may get a crowd for a time, but they will not comfort
the heart or satisfy the mind.

It cannot be successfully denied that the message of
the New Testament revelation has been the most re-
demptive power for human society men have ever
heard. When the gospel has been preached and believed something has happened—just as it happened
with a successful and keen business man when he took
Jesus home with him. He said, "Lord, if I have wronged
any man or taken unjustly from any man, I restore
unto him fourfold." And that decision of character
men have gained in every age when they have accepted
Jesus Christ.

Ability to understand all the mysteries of the agencies
at work, the person, death, and resurrection of Christ,
and the work of the Holy Spirit, or the problems of
Biblical criticism, is no more necessary to an intelligent acceptance of the facts than to say a man must
understand all the secrets of radio-activity before he
turns a dial on a radio. All the denunciation he might
hurl against the radio, all the denials he might make
about its possibilities, all refusal to test it out, would
be just as foolish as to say that he will not hearken to

the preaching of the gospel, or believe in its power, when he has not tried it.

What people want is a message that will meet their need. The gospel will do that. Nothing else will. Therefore, preach it. People will be prepared to hear a man who believes it, lives it, and preaches it.

I am not among those who say the people are not going to church. I believe they *are* going to church. The audiences in the churches may have been larger in some periods of history than at other periods, but taken time in and time out, where men proclaim the truth of God revealed in Christ, no institution records more constant and multitudinous attendance than the church within the past two years. I attended a meeting in a building in which the newspapers reported one of the great political conventions crowded thirty thousand people. If they had any more people than were there that day to hear the gospel and the report of its triumphs I do not know where they could have put them. But, men who were there and read the newspaper reports of the meeting the next morning were told that probably twenty thousand were present! In which case they told the truth about the actual number present, I have no means of knowing. I only know the newspapers are not prejudiced in their reports in favor of the Christian religion. I saw, for myself, a "capacity house" of listening humanity, eager to hear the gospel.

VI. *Finally, I say, audiences are prepared and* gather to hear men whose sincerity and experience of *the gospel they believe.* Sincerity is a precious quality of human personality—especially so in the preaching personality. It is like the window in a room otherwise without a light to banish its shadows. Through that window one may look and discern everything located in that room. So is sincerity. Motives can be read through it. There is no Jesuitical casuistry concealed in sincere personality. There are no ulterior motives hidden away there. There is no guile behind some high sounding phrases. There are only purity and cleanness, love, and conviction to determine word and action.

Sincerity is something that belongs to the man who loves God and his fellow-man. Such a man has no past record he fears may come out at unexpected moments. Take one illustration that happened more than twenty years ago when a minister enlisted in a fight to clean up the corruptions of his city. The agencies of that corruption were furious. They went back to the time and place of the preacher's youth and young manhood and dug up some old sins and follies with which he had then been charged. At a town meeting before the city council, the preacher appeared for the cause of righteousness. The opposition's orator paraded that preacher's past before the court and the people present. When he had finished, the preacher was called on to defend himself, if he could! He gladly improved the opportunity by saying what the opposition stated was only about half true. They did not tell all that described him in those days! He then proceeded to tell what they had left out but which was known to the official board of his church. But, said he, "that was more than twenty years ago when I was the same kind of sinner as the men who confront and oppose me now. It was before I found Jesus Christ as my Savior." He had nothing to hide, the blood of Christ cleansed him of those sins, and from that day to the hour of this arraignment he tried to walk in the light as He is in the light. The people knew this to be so and they filled and continue to fill the auditorium where he preaches. The truth he had believed was not something he had learned with his head, but as John Oman would say, "a view of things human and divine which is a central and essential part of yourself."[4] He was sincere, an Israelite of the Spirit in whom there was no guile.

Sincerity not only describes a state of purity and cleanness from all corruption, deception, or hypocrisy; but it is also a dynamic, a force that gives impact to what a man says when he expresses his thought and belief. Without doubt it may give force to many a false concept and dangerous purpose. As a man returns to his Book and the story of the apostle Paul's life, he cannot escape the conviction that he was sincere when he breathed out threatening and slaughter against the early disciples of Jesus. He "verily thought (he) was doing God service." I would be the last of all men to bring the charge of insincerity against those who in unbelief disparage the claims Christians make for the authority of Biblical truth or who make intellectual sport of the simplicity of Christian teaching and faith. I have too many acquaintances through books and social contacts to fall into that pit or to lead young men in the gospel ministry to fall into it. But the genuineness in those who have rejected this faith is what those who believe think makes them dangerous. There is persuasion, power, in sincerity. When sincerity is founded on the truth, has been motivated by righteousness and love for God and our fellow-man, it also gains in power and impact upon the minds and hearts of men when it utters the gospel.

It is soon discovered whether a man is sincere. Its validation of personality is inevitable. People respect and honor such men and by that perception they are prepared to listen when they preach. If sincerity is backed with intelligence, knowledge of the ways of God with men, culture of the mind and heart, and love, people will go prepared to hear the message that is uttered.

NOTES

Foreword

1. Anonymous, *The Art of Candidating*. Boston; Horace Worth; 1907. pp. 35-36
2. Dabney, Robert, *Sacred Rhetoric*. New York; Anson, D. F.; Randolph and Co., 1870. pp. 139-140

Chapter I

1. Covert, William Chalmers, *Facing Our Day*. New York; Abingdon Press; 1934. p. 23
2. Krutch, Joseph Wood, *The Modern Temper*. New York; Harcourt Brace and Company; 1934. p. 45
3. Oman, John, *Concerning the Ministry*. New York; Harper and Brothers; 1937. p. 45
4. Seebohn, Chapter X, p. 8. Reference to Carlyle—Chartism
5. Sheppard, H. R. L., *The Impatience of a Parson*. New York; Doubleday, Doran and Company, Inc.; 1928

Chapter II

1. Vinet, *Homiletics or Theory of Preaching*. Edinburgh; T. and T. Clark; Second edition
2. Broadus, John A., *Preparation and Delivery of Sermons*. New York; Richard R. Smith, Inc.; 1930. pp. 22-23
3. *The Confession of Faith* (Presbyterian Church, U.S.A.)
4. Davis, Ozora S., *Principles of Preaching*. Chicago; The University of Chicago Press; 1924. p. 192
5. *Ibid.*; note p. 186
6. Dale, R. W., *Nine Lectures on Preaching*. New York; A. S. Barnns; 1878. p. 230
7. Buttrick, George A., *Jesus Came Preaching*. New York; Charles Scribners Sons; 1931. p. 149

Chapter III

1. Buttrick, George A., *op. cit.*; p. 152
2. Ruskin, John, *Hortus Inclusus—Praeterita*. Boston; Aldine Publishing Co.; pp. 282-283
3. Johnson, Herrick, *The Ideal Ministry*. New York; Fleming H. Revell Co.; 1908. p. 52

Chapter IV

1. Johnson, Herrick, *op. cit.*; p. 314
2. Hoyt, Arthur S., *The Work of Preaching*. New York; Macmillan Co.; 1909. p. 98
3. Breed, David R., *Preparing to Preach*. New York; Hodder and Stoughton; 1911. p. 60
4. Davis, Ozora S., *op. cit.*; pp. 201-202
5. *Ibid.*; p. 200
6. Breed, David R., *op. cit.*; p. 377
7. Johnson, Herrick, *op. cit.*; p. 261
8. Faber, F. W., *All of Jesus*

Chapter V

1. Broadus, John A., *op. cit.*; p. 270
2. *Ibid.*; note p. 273
3. Lyman, A. J., *Preaching in the New Age*. New York; Fleming H. Revell; 1902. p. 108
4. Broadus, John A., *op. cit.*; p. 267
5. Davis, Ozora S., *op. cit.*; p. 210
6. Johnson, Herrick, *op. cit.*; pp. 377-378
7. Breed, David R., *Preparing to Preach*
8. Dabney, Robert, *op. cit.*; p. 144
9. Dale, R. W., *op. cit.*
10. Broadus, John A., *op. cit.*; p. 256
11. Johnson, Herrick, *op. cit.*; pp. 380-381
12. Phillips, Harold Cook, *Seeing the Invisible*. New York; Harper and Brothers; 1932
13. Hough, Lynn Harold, *The University of Experience*. New York; Harper and Brothers; 1932

Chapter VI

1. Hoyt, Arthur S., *op. cit.*
2. Bradford, Gamaliel, *The Journal of Gamaliel Bradford*; New York; Houghton Mifflin Co.; 1933. p. 493

Chapter VII

1. Johnson, Herrick, *op. cit.*; p. 385
2. *Ibid.*; p. 385
3. Breed, David R., *op. cit.*; p. 112

Chapter VIII

1. Broadus, John A., *op. cit.*; p. 207
2. Allen, A. V. G., *Life and Letters of Phillips Brooks* (3 vols.). New York; E. P. Dutton and Co.; 1901. vol. ii.; p. 243

Chapter IX

1. Beecher, Henry Ward, *Yale Lectures on Preaching.* New York; Fords Howard and Hulbert; 1899. p. 299
2. Oman, John, *op. cit.*; p. 207
3. Gossip, Arthur John, *In Christ's Stead*, The Warrack Lectures. New York; Hodder and Stoughton; 1925. p. 190
4. Gossip, *The Galilean Accent.* pp. 115-116
5. Gossip, *On the Edge of the Crowd.* pp. 290-291
6. Gossip, *In Christ's Stead.* pp. 193-194
7. Crocker, Lionel, *Henry Ward Beecher's Art of Preaching;* Chicago; The University of Chicago Press; 1934. p. 145
8. Gossip, *In Christ's Stead.* pp. 190-191

Chapter X

1. Broadus, John A., *Preparation and Delivery of Sermons*
2. Johnson, Herrick, *The Ideal Ministry*

Chapter XII

1. Pattison, T. Harwood, *The History of Christian Preaching.* Philadelphia; American Baptist Publication Society; 1909. p. 1
2. *Ibid.*; p. 4
3. Morgan, G. Campbell, *Preaching.* New York; Fleming H. Revell Co.; 1937. pp. 11-12
4. Pattison, *op. cit.*; p. 5
5. Phelps, Austin, *Theory of Preaching.* New York; Charles Scribners Sons; 1881. p. 1
6. Whately, *Elements of Rhetoric.* New York; Sheldon and Company; 1828
7. Brastow, *op. cit.*; p. 25
8. Brooks, Phillips, *Lectures on Preaching.* New York; E. P. Dutton and Co.; 1877. p. 8

9. Gossip, A. J., *In Christ's Stead.* p. 15
10. Johnson, Herrick, *op. cit.;* p. 280
11. Phelps, Austin, *op. cit.;* p. 28
12. Lipsky, Abraham, *John Wesley — A Portrait.* New York; Simon and Schuster; 1928. p. 26
13. *Webster's New Dictionary.* Springfield, Mass.; G. and C. Merriam Company; 1930
14. Buttrick, George A., *op. cit.;* pp. 7, 75

Chapter XIII

1. Cadman, S. Parkes, *Ambassadors of God.* New York; Macmillan Company; 1920. p. 99
2. *Bulletin of Theta Phi;* June, 1937
3. Forsyth, Peter Taylor, *Positive Preaching and the Modern Mind.* New York; A. C. Armstrong and Son; 1907. pp. 41-42
4. *The Bible; an American Translation.* The University of Chicago Press; 1935
5. Hoyt, Arthur S., *op. cit.;* pp. 10-12
6. Buttrick, George A., *op. cit.;* p. 7
7. *The Presbyterian Banner.* September 24, 1936
8. Horne, Sylvester, *The Romance of Preaching.* New York; Fleming H. Revell Company; 1914. p. 29
9. Sheppard, H. R. L., *The Impatience of a Parson.* New York; Doubleday, Doran and Company; 1928
10. Crocker, Lionel, *Henry Ward Beecher's Speaking Art.* p. 93

Chapter XV

1. Lowell, James Russell, *On Board the '76*
2. Coe, George A., *What is Christian Education?* New York; Charles Scribners Sons; 1929. p. 69
3. Buttrick, George A., *op. cit.;* pp. 118-141
4. Oman, John, *op. cit.;* p. 36

Chapter XVI

1. Cairns, Frank, *The Prophet of the Heart.* New York; Harper and Brothers; 1935. p. 5
2. Proverbs 20:27
3. Zorbaugh, Harry W., *The Gold Coast and the Slums.* Chicago; The University of Chicago Press; 1935

4. Redwood, Hugh, *God in the Slums.* New York; Fleming H. Revell Company; 1931

5. Lamentations 1: 2, 12

6. Horne, Sylvester, *op. cit.;* p. 170

Chapter XVII

1. Hoyt, Arthur S., *op. cit.*

2. Cabell, Robert H., *Good Will.* Armours (magazine) March, 1937

3. Lippman, Walter, *A Preface to Morals.* New York; The Macmillan Company; 1929. p. 48

4. Oman, John, *op. cit.;* p. 38

Notes

Notes

Notes